After Alinsky:
Community Organizing in Illinois

After Alinsky:
Community Organizing in Illinois

Edited by Peg Knoepfle
with an Interview of Tom Gaudette

Illinois Issues
Sangamon State University
Springfield, Illinois

This publication was made possible by a grant
from the Woods Charitable Fund, Inc.

Printed in the United States of America

Cover design by Larz Gaydos

Photo of roundtable discussion on page 123 © Lucia Woods 1989

Library of Congress Catalog Card Number: Pending
ISBN: 0-9620873-3-5

The first nine chapters of this book appeared in *Illinois Issues* as a series of articles on
community organizing, funded by Woods Charitable Fund, Inc. The articles were
published from January 1988 through July 1989.

For those who've grown old and stayed
young empowering their communities

Chapter Photos

Page 1
Witty, intelligent, tough and a deep believer in the right and ability of people to determine their own destiny, Saul Alinsky, 1909-1972, is known as the father of community organizing.

Page 11
Pilsen, just southwest of the Loop, is a traditional port of entry for Chicago's Mexican immigrants.

Page 23
Neighbors stop to chat in Cragin on Chicago's northwest side, not far from the offices of the Save Our Neighborhoods/Save Our City Coalition.

Page 35
Deacon Lee, president of Developing Communities Project, addresses a meeting at Reformation Lutheran Church. The result was the creation of a network to tutor at-risk high school students.

Page 41
Worried tenants seek answers about pending evictions at a citywide conference of Federal Housing Authority tenants held in February 1988.

Page 53
Gale Cincotta (left) is executive director of the National Training and Information Center and chairperson of National People's Action, both based in Chicago. Heather Booth (right) is president of Chicago's Midwest Academy and of Citizen Action, headquartered in Washington, D.C.

Page 61
One-third of the suburban, ranch-style houses stand empty in Beacon Hill, a run-down neighborhood in Chicago Heights where the Chicago Area Project has established a presence.

Page 71
During the 1980s depopulation of the Illinois countryside continued as farms and businesses folded, and young people moved away in search of better opportunities.

Page 83
Mayor Harold Washington (center) breaks the ground on November 25, 1987, for 70 townhouses to be developed by the Kenwood-Oakland Community Organization (KOCO). Standing to the left of the mayor is KOCO's executive director Robert L. Lucas; on the right is Ald. Timothy C. Evans. The ceremony was Washington's last official action; he died later that day.

Page 97
Chicago organizer Tom Gaudette started out as president of the Chatham Community Council in the 1950s, then went on to work with Saul Alinsky, organize in Chicago and mentor leaders and organizers nationwide.

Page 123
Paul M. Green (center) emphasizes a point. To his left are Cheryl Frank and Barak Obama; to his right is Christopher Robert Reed.

Contents

Acknowledgments

This book was made possible by a grant from the Woods Charitable Fund, Inc. and by the personal generosity of more people than I can name — a generosity that reflects their own deep commitment to the neighborhoods and communities whose stories are told in this book. I owe special thanks to Ken Rolling and Bob Gannett for their encouragement and help and to all the authors for being teachers and talkers as well as writers. I owe Tom Gaudette for sharing his stories of organizing and Debi Edmund for transcribing and editing them, John Kretzmann for doing a brilliant job as moderator of the roundtable discussion, and the publications staff for their care and creativity. I owe Mike Lennon and Caroline Gherardini and my fellow workers at *Illinois Issues* for getting me into this and keeping me at it. And most of all I owe John Knoepfle, who said he'd stand by me no matter what and did so on numerous occasions.

Cover Photos

Front cover: starting at the top right and going clockwise.

Mary Gonzales, then associate director of UNO of Chicago and director of Pilsen Neighbors Community Council; now director of Pilsen Neighbors Community Council. *Photo by Jon Randolph.*

Carolers from Champaign County Health Care Consumers demonstrate at Carle Clinic in December 1985. From left to right: Jim Duffett, Health Care Consumers director Mike Doyle, Diane Miesenhelter, John Lee Johnson and Keith Irvin. *Photo courtesy of Champaign County Health Care Consumers.*

Farmers demonstrate at the State House in 1978. *Photo courtesy of Illinois Issues.*

A member of Northside Action Council of Peoria demonstrates for lower taxes. *Photo courtesy of Illinois Issues.*

SON/SOC leaders Jean Mayer and Joyce Zick at 1988 hearings on home equity in the State of Illinois Center in Chicago. *Photo by Jon Randolph.*

Nancy B. Jefferson, civil rights leader and chief executive officer and president of the Midwest Community Council, at the council's 1985 fundraising dinner. *Photo Courtesy of Midwest Community Council.*

Back cover: starting at top right and going clockwise:

Bethel New Life Community Development Organization begins work in December 1985 to transform an old public school building in West Garfield Park into a Living Learning Center. At the celebration are Mayor Harold Washington (center) and Bethel director Mary L. Nelson (far right). *Photo courtesy of Bethel New Life.*

Gale Cincotta addresses the November 1988 National Conference on Initiatives for Affordable Housing, sponsored by the National Training and Information Center. *Photo by Paul L. Merideth.*

David Del Valle, an organizer for Northwest Community Organization, holds a sign that Commonwealth Edison used to mark PCB sites being cleaned up in Chicago neighborhoods in 1988. *Photo by Thom Clark.*

Two youngsters ham it up outside the storefront that the Chicago Area Project is using as headquarters for its Chicago Heights Community Committee. *Photo by Paul Beaty.*

This abandoned Cook County Housing Authority building in Ford Heights is being converted into a Chicago Area Project youth center. *Photo by Paul Beaty.*

Introduction

The title of this book is deliberately ambiguous. *After Alinsky: Community Organizing in Illinois* implies a continuity and a durability that are becoming increasingly evident. But it also points to changes that have occurred since 1939 when Saul Alinsky invented a new kind of organizing in Chicago's Back of the Yards and since 1961 when he became front page news again by organizing Woodlawn. Finally, *After Alinsky* indicates the presence of other organizing traditions that do not derive from Alinsky's model but developed parallel to it. Civil rights organizing, for instance, which dominates the century and influenced the efforts of all other ethnic groups in the U.S. and worldwide. Or the Baker Brownell/Richard Poston community development model, which made Southern Illinois University in Carbondale an international center for community-based development during the 1950s and early '60s and earned Richard Poston the title of "doctor of sick towns."

Illinoisans tend to have a fragmentary knowledge of the history of their own state, its people and its communities. That is why working on the articles that make up this book was more a journey of discovery than an editing job. The more I learned, the more I wanted to find out. And the more I found out, the more I wanted the authors to present a panoramic view of organizing in Illinois, or at least a series of different cuts on the subject. I hope that this book will help readers see Illinois community organizing in its diversity and perhaps come to some conclusions about its purposes and processes. And its importance. As Barak Obama points out in the final chapter: ". . . organizing has a long tradition in this country. It didn't start with Alinsky. It didn't stop with Alinsky. What it has to do with is: How do you include the excluded in this country? And its history started with the founding fathers."

Continuity and durability. Ben Joravsky lines it out: ". . . the Alinsky model of a democratically run, church-based community organization has become the prototype for groups in poor and working-class black, white-ethnic and Hispanic neighborhoods." Tom Gaudette translates those words into events and people, revealing the drama, the creativity, the comedy of organizing. Wilfredo Cruz takes us into Chicago's Mexican-American neighborhoods and their Catholic churches to show us the United Neighborhood Organization at a crucial moment in its development. Paul M. Green poses the question: Can white ethnics organize in a racially changing city without being labeled bigots? Green talks about race, money and politics and about attempts to achieve "a strange hopeful alliance" between Chicago Mayor Harold Washington and these white-ethnic working-class communities. The subject is taken up again in the concluding chapter, excerpts from a many-faceted roundtable discussion.

In "Neighbors and Tenants fight HUD and ComEd" Thom Clark details how two well-established Alinsky-style organizations on Chicago's north side won battles by doing effective research, making coalitions and getting good media coverage. He also indicates the growing importance of tenants' rights organizations in the struggle for affordability in housing and diversity in neighborhoods.

But *After Alinsky,* as Joravsky tells us, is also a story of bitter disappointment, reassessment and change. Alinksy-style organizing and the civil rights movement, both strong in Chicago, failed to prevent racial polarization, white flight and economic decay. As a result, there was a tendency to turn away from Alinsky's broad-based, generalist organizing with its emphasis on building "indigenous leadership." Social activists began building coalitions on issues at the city, state and national level. They got involved in electoral politics, making mayoral history in Chicago and sending new people like Ald. Luis Gutierrez, state Sen. Miguel del Valle (D-5, Chicago) and U.S. Rep. Lane Evans (D-17, Rock Island) to the Chicago City Council, the General Assembly and Congress. And, as Cheryl Frank reports, Chicago organizers began talking to people downstate.

Thus Patrick Barry shows how Gale Cincotta moved from organizing on Chicago's west side to waging war against the banking industry, followed by negotiations and new partnerships. And how Heather Booth moved from being a working mother and a former activist to building a national base for a new "populist-progressive" electoral majority.

Meanwhile, in low- and moderate-income Chicago neighborhoods survival was, and still is, the basic concern. During the 1970s and '80s some Alinsky-style organizations became staff-directed providers of social services or created nonprofit corporations to develop neighborhood economies. The risk: mismanagement and loss of purpose and independence. The need: to stay alive. The hope: to build an economy that is more diverse, more efficient and maybe more sustainable than the one that has produced two decades of deindustrialization, neighborhood abandonment and disinvestment.

In a doctoral thesis cited in the bibliography, South Shore Bank executive Michael Bennett traces the "devolving roles" of community organizations from advocacy to service provision and economic development. In the roundtable discussion Clark notes that some of the programs forced on banks by the Community Reinvestment Act have proved to be profitable to the banks rather than merely charitable to the neighborhoods. And Barak Obama ponders political empowerment, economic self-sufficiency and community organizing. He concludes that the first two, necessary as they are, will not succeed in bettering the lot of oppressed people without the grass-roots involvement and leadership that only organizing can nurture. A plurality of problems requires a plurality of solutions.

Cheryl Frank reaches the same conclusion in her extensive research on downstate organizing. She also deals with a plurality of organizing traditions. Among them is Alinsky's — alive and well downstate through the efforts of Shel Trapp from the National Training and Information Center and the connections with the Midwest Academy and Illinois Public Action (formerly called Illinois Public Action Council) — not to mention the United Auto Workers in Danville and Vincent Thomas's feisty Community Action Program in Rock Island.

But Frank also talks about civil rights activism in the courts and on the streets that changed the form of city government in Springfield. And about Richard Poston's model for community development that he is now applying, with the help of white and African-American leadership, in Cairo. Health care, groundwater, farm foreclosures and the underground media are among the subjects Frank touches on, as she explains issues and coalitions that will confront Springfield and Washington in the 1990s.

Bill Kemp focuses on some of the poorest communities in the nation, little-known pockets of poverty in Chicago's diverse, energetic and vastly underrated south suburbs. He tells of efforts by the Chicago Area Project — founded in the 1930s by Alinsky's mentor and rival, Clifford Shaw — to create a better environment for youth. But these neighborhoods are so ravaged by deindustrialization, family dissolution and crime that there are few institutions left for organizers to build on. Kemp asks if organizing can help communities that seem to lack everything, including the two fundamentals: family support and jobs.

In "Bedrock Democracy: Community Organizations and Washington's Civic Legacy" Christopher Robert Reed speaks of a plurality of empowerments: civic, political and economic. Reversing Obama's equation, he points out that community organizing alone does not create true empowerment. There must also be full participation in the "political economy." He says that for Mayor Harold Washington "bedrock democracy" meant using his power as mayor to make community groups and their constituents "partners in the process of economic development." Thus inclusiveness becomes the bedrock on which to rebuild a city — or a nation.

An axiom emerges from the stories and discussions in this book: Building civic, economic and political participation requires long-term commitment. New options are also apparent: Community organizing is capable of breaking up what Obama calls "ideological gridlock" by appealing to the concerns of both liberals and conservatives. But participation in general and community organizing in particular are, by nature, full of conflicts. Power, as Alinsky said, is what is being dealt with here.

Along this line of thought, I have listed several books by Harry Boyte in the bibliography. I have done this, first of all, because he retrieves so many of the nation's and Illinois' democratic traditions — an antidote to the "cultural weightlessness" that Norman Birnbaum describes so convincingly in *Radical Renewal*. But Boyte also outlines the unresolved conflicts in these traditions, in particular in a collection of essays he edited with Frank Riessman enititled *The New Populism*. In one of the essays, for example, Cornel West, an African-American socialist, points out that he does not share the populist faith in the good will of the American people since both the Emancipation Proclamation and the *Brown vs. Board of Education* decision were "far removed" from popular approval and would have lost if put to a referendum. And feminist Elizabeth Kasmarck Minnich warns that populism must not only affirm diversity "but concentrate on differences," avoiding in its effort to be inclusive the superficial pluralism that says — "we can all be in this together because really we are all alike despite all our apparent differences." Respecting even concentrating on differences in order to foster a democratic polity may be what the authors of *After Alinsky* are talking about as they puzzle over the relationships between Illinois' community organizations and its political movements, between race and ethnicity, and among the various forms of empowerment — civic, political and economic.

From a journalist's point of view, the excitement of working on this book was that the stories never stopped breaking. Updates would require another volume, but a few are needed to fill in some gaps. Currently, the major organizing story in Chicago is school reform, perhaps the most inclusive civic action the city has ever undertaken. And one that began in the city's homes and neighborhoods. Among the neighborhoods whose stories are not told in this book are Chicago's Asian communities, yet their task in school reform is particularly complex and epitomizes the long-term, all-encompassing commitment that school reform requires. More will be heard from these communities in the coming decade.

Another concern is housing. As of the spring of 1990, the *Buena* case, whose Uptown beginnings are recounted by Thom Clark, was on appeal. The tenants' organizations had won the first round in their efforts to uphold a congressional moratorium on prepaying FHA-financed mortgages, and Housing and Urban Development Secy. Jack Kemp was backing Congress rather than the landlords on the moratorium issue. Kemp had also approved the purchase and tenant management of another FHA-financed Uptown apartment building, and community organizations across the city were talking to each other about evictions, gentrification and ways to finance affordable housing. The Statewide Housing Coalition, composed of Chicago, suburban and downstate groups, was monitoring implementation of the Affordable Housing Trust Fund, which it helped pass in 1989, and working on other statewide problems, such as tenants' rights. According to Clark: "Housing will be the key issue of the 1990s. If there is such a thing as an omnibus housing bill out of Congress, all the groups will get behind it."

Meanwhile, a new financing opportunity for nonprofit housing development corporations throughout the U.S was provided by 1989 amendments to the federal savings and loans bailout. Besides making it easier for community groups to monitor whether banks and savings and loans are investing in poor and working-class neighborhoods, the amendments give the nonprofits access to low-interest mortgage rates on properties foreclosed on by failed savings and loans. The amendments had the backing of U.S. Rep. Henry Gonzalez (D-20, Texas), Rev. Jesse Jackson and of an organization with Alinsky roots that is mentioned but not covered at length in this book: American Communities Organized for Reform Now (ACORN). Organizing locally and working for social change nationally, ACORN has Chicago branches in Englewood and North Lawndale. Affordable housing, school reform and campaigns for better law enforcement and tougher prosecution of rape cases have been its issues in Chicago. The latter campaign brought together women from all parts of the city.

In troubled East St. Louis, the Metro East Church and Community Organization (MECCO) was working this spring on the city's garbage crisis and its drug problems. Founded in 1988, the Alinsky-style organization consists of 16 churches and seven church-related organizations. Developing an educated citizenry that can shape its own destiny is MECCO's goal.

Some updates on organizations covered in the book: In Chicago a reorganized United Neighborhood Organization (UNO) with Danny Solis at the helm "wants to play a leading role on a range of quality-of-life issues," according to UNO organizer Phil Mullins. The issues are affordable housing, school reform and health care. UNO will try to use what it learned in Chicago school reform as a model for restructuring health care. Mary Gonzales, who left UNO and is now executive director of Pilsen Neighbors Community Council, says that both the council and the community are deeply involved in school reform. But Pilsen also feels targeted by gentrification. Currently 75 percent of the homes there are owner-occupied; the council wants to keep them that way and to help people from the community become home owners. It has formed its own housing development corporation to build affordable housing on vacant land.

Developing Communities Project (DCP) in Chicago's Greater Roseland Area has grown from seven to 14 churches. With a grant from the Illinois Department of Alcohol and Substance Abuse it is taking an "ecological" approach in its efforts to prevent drug and alcohol abuse. This includes organizing to halt the granting of liquor licenses, better enforcement against drug houses and alternative programs for youth to understand the dangers of drugs and to improve their self-esteem. DCP's effort can stand for many in Illinois and across the nation — a frontline, grass-roots initiative to prevent both drug abuse and the wholesale criminalization and imprisonment of minority and low-income youth.

Heather Booth, now heading Citizen Action in Washington, D.C., says her organization has targeted five additional states in its direct mail campaign. Global warming and the environment, universal health care and insurance reform are the issues she sees looming in the 1990s. Back in Chicago, National People's Action director Gale Cincotta says she's "hot to trot" on the peace bonus. Money that would have gone to military spending should go for housing and jobs, she says.

In the south suburbs, Chicago Area Project's new youth center in Ford Heights was scheduled to open in April, and in Elgin its new program for Cambodian youth was underway with help from local and state agencies. The South Suburban Action Conference (SSAC), now 30 churches strong with an African-American, white and Hispanic membership, got an agreement in January from the Southwest Board of Realtors and the Greater South Suburban Board of Realtors to create joint access and multiple listing services and not to engage in the "steering" of minorities to certain areas. SSAC and the realtors had been negotiating since 1987.

Downstate, the Pembroke Area Concerned Citizens and the farmers using irrigation systems negotiated with each other after four years of confrontation and came up with a compromise legislative proposal for adequate wells in Pembroke. The legislation was vetoed twice by Gov. James R. Thompson, but $100,000 for Pembroke's wells was included in the governor's fiscal 1991 budget under Lt. Gov. George Ryan's rural development program.

The Champaign County Health Care Consumers joined with other community groups to create a statewide Campaign for Better Health Care. Chicago and downstate organizations were meeting regularly on local health concerns and backing proposed state legislation for universal health care, modeled on the Canadian system. The Illinois Stewardship Alliance, formerly Illinois South, was backing federal family farm legislation and expressing increased concern over the environmental effects of long-wall coal mining. And the low-watt radio station, owned and operated by Springfield tenants' rights activist Dewayne Readus, had become a national First Amendment issue. For an update, see the articles by Rich Shereikis cited in the bibliography.

Finally, beyond all these events and actions there is another, deeper aspect to organizing. Call it values, culture, spirit — whatever you want. You can see it in the stories in this book. In Cruz's account of the changes UNO brings to participants' lives and to their estimation of themselves. In Green's story of SON/SOC trying to define and negotiate its true self interest. In Hank De Zutter's story, cited in the bibliography, of Mary Johnson Volpe and the Northeast Austin Organization. In Reed's description of the network of block clubs and the years of commitment and struggle on Chicago's south and west sides. There is hope here and hard work. Obama probably sums it up best when he describes how organizing enriches the organizer and how it moves marginalized people into the mainstream, causing that mainstream "to get rich and examine and remake itself."

Alinsky's Legacy

by Ben Joravsky

*'Alinsky lives. His concepts
are universal to organizing.'*
Ed Chambers

 is already placed. Photo courtesy of the Industrial Areas Foundation

T he old folks remember Saul Alinsky from the early days as the gawky, bookish-looking fellow in the round-rim glasses, who stood at the back of meeting rooms, quietly and inconspicuously taking notes. That was in 1939, the year Alinsky and his colleague Joseph Meegan put together the Back of the Yards Neighborhood Council, an effort to transform a rundown, working-class slum on the south side of Chicago. None of them could have expected, or even imagined, the sweeping consequences of that birth. "How could they have known what they were creating? Who could have predicted it?" says Robert Slayton, historian and author of *Back of the Yards: The Making of a Local Democracy*. "But even now, when I go to community meetings, and I hear people talking about neighborhood empowerment and controlling one's destiny, I think, 'My God, that's Alinsky.' And it all goes back to the Back of the Yards."

Now, of course, Alinsky's influence is beyond refute. He died in 1972 of a heart attack, but the Alinsky model of a democratically run, church-based community organization has become the prototype for groups in poor and working-class black, white-ethnic and Hispanic neighborhoods across the country.

The organizers he trained — Tom Gaudette, Fred Ross Sr., and Ed Chambers chief among them — in turn trained others, including Cesar Chavez, cofounder of the United Farmworkers Union. Their influence has shaped movements of politics, labor, peace and civil rights. In 1940 Alinsky created the Industrial Areas Foundation, a training school for organizers. Now under Chambers' command, it oversees a network of 22 organizations in regions as disparate as New York, Texas and southern California.

Even activists such as Heather Booth and Shel Trapp, who never or only briefly met Alinsky, have been touched by his philosophy. Local leadership, confrontational tactics, personalizing the issue — all well-recognized and

Ben Joravsky has been covering neighborhood issues in *The Chicago Reporter* and the *Reader* for many years. He has also coauthored two books with Eduardo Camacho: *Race and Politics in Chicago* and, most recently, *Against the Tide: The Middle Class in Chicago*. "Community organizing: Alinsky's legacy" was first published in the January 1988 *Illinois Issues*.

widely practiced tenets taught by Booth and Trapp at their training schools in Chicago — were espoused for the first time in *Reveille for Radicals* and *Rules for Radicals*, the two primers Alinksy wrote. And through it all, he developed almost a personality cult of admirers, young and old, galvanized by his persona: the caustic, acerbic and witty University of Chicago graduate who scored scholars and academicians and struck a pose of street-smart tough.

"I remember my first meeting with Saul," says Peter Martinez, an organizer who was trained and employed by Alinsky and later helped organize the United Neighborhood Organization (UNO), a network of groups active in Chicago's Hispanic community. "He said, 'Have you been to college?' I said, 'Yes.' He said, 'Oh, Hell. Have you graduated?' I said, 'Yes.' He said, 'Things are really going downhill. What's your major?' I said, 'English.' So, he said: 'Thank God, if you had said social work or sociology, I'd have kicked your ass out the door.'"

Not surprisingly, it is in Chicago, Alinsky's hometown, that his thumb print is strongest. Indeed, his organizations were tailored for Chicago. They were rooted in neighborhood parishes, organized around union principles of solidarity, and dedicated to the steel-edged proposition that power — in this case the city's Democratic machine — concedes nothing unless it has to.

"Chicago is the Harvard of community organizing," says John McDermott, former publisher of *The Chicago Reporter*. "Or, maybe I should say the Notre Dame of organizing, since the Catholic church has played such an integral role." By the late 1970s, the number of active, Alinsky-style organizations here hovered near 100. Now that number may have halved, the result no doubt of suburban migration and inner city deterioration, the very things the organizations were formed to prevent. Some of Alinsky's best-known creations have folded. Others, like The Woodlawn Organization (TWO), which helped stabilize a poor, south-side, black community in the 1960s, are now known more for social service and development efforts than agitation.

More and more, the talk in town is that Alinsky's pot-boiling tactics of confrontation are passe and no longer unnerve or intimidate egregious corporations, landlords or politicians. Instead, many activists say the time has come to forge partnerships with corporate Chicago and seed the inner city with philanthropic donations that will sprout not-for-profit housing and small-business operations.

Many of the best and brightest community activists have run for office, usually as allies of the late Mayor Harold Washington. Some — such as Aldermen Luis Gutierrez (26th Ward), Dorothy Tillman (3rd) and Bobby Rush (2nd) — even got elected. And, ironically, they sometimes scolded the spunkier organizations such as UNO and the Northwest Neighborhood Federation for embarrassing Washington with their boisterous demonstrations.

Doubt still exists about Alinsky's approach to organizing, most of it the same criticism that nagged him while he lived. His approach, critics say, is too simplistic. It avoids confronting racism, breeds parochialism, shies from electoral politics and sets such fundamentally routine and meaningless goals for its followers that the power structure remains unshaken, and the poor are provided with what amounts to some sort of recreational diversion.

"Alinsky's organizations are not made for structural change," says Don Rose, a veteran Chicago political strategist, who has been active in civil rights, anti-machine and progressive causes. "He used the rhetoric of radicalism for the purpose of entree to the system. His client, by and large, was the church. And the church is interested in pacification, not change."

All of such criticism, Alinsky's supporters counter, misses the point. Organizing is a process by which exploited people learn to employ the tools of a democratic society, which one day will have no choice but to accept them as equal members. "Alinsky lives," says Chambers. "His concepts are universal to organizing. We have developed them, of course. We have made them better. But his fundamental principles will never change."

The man himself was born in 1909 on Chicago's west side. The facts of his early life are based mostly on his own recollections — a somewhat faulty source, given Alinsky's passion for embellishment. In a now-famous 1965 interview with Marion Sanders for *Harper's Magazine*, Alinsky recalls a childhood spent as a Jewish street ruffian who battled gangs of Irish and Poles. When he was a teenager, his parents divorced. For years, Alinsky shuttled back and forth between his mother in Chicago and his father, a businessman in Los Angeles. His first taste of poverty came even before the Depression.

"My problem was eating," Alinsky told *Harper's*. "I knew my mother would gladly give me her last dollar and the last crumbs on her table. But she was having a hard time and my father had more or less disappeared from sight. So I'd tell her I had enough. I could have gone on a relief project. But I don't know why this is — I'll steal before I'll take charity. . . .

"I entered the University of Chicago in 1926. More or less by accident, I majored in archeology and I fell in love with the subject. It was all very exciting and dramatic to me. The artifacts were not just pieces of stone or clay. My imagination could carry me back to the past so that when I stood in front of an old Inca altar, I could hear the cries of human sacrifice. You need a lot of imagination to be a good organizer. Today when I go into a community, I suffer and resent with the people there, and they feel this."

In 1930 he won a scholarship from the university and enrolled in its graduate school of criminology, where he elected as an independent study to conduct field research on Al Capone's gangsters. One year later, restless with academia, he dropped out of school and went to work for Clifford R. Shaw's Institute of Juvenile Research. It was Shaw who in 1939 directed Alinsky to the Back of the Yards, with instructions to determine how the community might eradicate a wave of juvenile crime.

"I think it would be a mistake to say that Alinsky went into the Back of the Yards, and just started a community organization," says Sandford Horwitt, a historian whose biography of Alinsky will be published this year. "I think he had some general ideas of what he wanted to do. But the specifics evolved from his experiences."

"This was Upton Sinclair's jungle," Alinsky said of the community. "This was not the slum across the tracks, this was the slum across the tracks from across the tracks." That description is a bit misleading. True, the overcrowded community of crumbling wood shanties and tenements bordered on the city's filthy stockyards. But it also bustled with organizational activity. There were dozens of civic, youth and religious organizations, not to mention stockyard union activists, whose heroics fired Alinsky's imagination.

"The union organizers Alinsky found working in the Back of the Yards were professional radicals," David Fink wrote in his book, *The Radical Vision of Saul Alinsky.* "Their specific assignment from CIO boss [John L.] Lewis was to organize Chicago's packinghouse workers. To accomplish this . . . . involved agitation — convincing people that their problems were not unique, but connected with the problems of poor, exploited people everywhere. They preached unity, solidarity, action and reform. Alinsky went to [their] mass meetings. The organizers fascinated him."

The vision of powerless people uniting to shape their destiny stirred Alinsky. He related it to larger struggles in Europe against Hitler, Mussolini, fascism and anti-Semitism. "I went in there to fight fascism," Alinsky told *Harper's.* "Delinquency was just incidental, the real crime was fascism. If you had asked me then what my profession was, I would have told you I was a professional anti-fascist."

It struck him as almost hopelessly pathetic that the poor laborers of Packingtown, as the area was called, were divided into feuding ethnic camps of Poles, Irish and Lithuanians. To preach unity, however, on the basis of brotherhood and harmony would be naive, Alinsky figured. No one would listen; their hostile passions ran too deep. He would have to prove that ethnic rivalries thwarted their own self-interest. "To succeed, Alinsky and Meegan had to convince each faction of the notion of greater good," says Slayton. "They would say, 'Okay, for 30 days a month you can hate each other. But on the last day, you are brothers, no matter what.'"

"In the world as it is, man moves primarily because of self interest," Alinsky wrote in *Reveille For Radicals.* "In the world as it is, the right things are usually done for the wrong reason." Or, as he later told *Harper's:* "I never appealed to people on the basis of abstract values. . . . Sure, everybody's against sin, but you're not going to get off your prat to do anything about it. To the Catholic priests my approach was simply this: 'You're telling your people to stay out of the CIO because it's Communist-dominated. . . . So what do they do? They say, 'Yes, father,' and walk out of your church and join the union. [Why?] Because those union people are doing something about their living problems. . . .while you sit on your rear end in your sacristy.' "

The Back of the Yards council's first meeting was in July 1939. All totaled, 350 people attended, representing 76 organizations. Bishop Bernard Sheil, auxiliary archbishop of the Archdiocese, was elected honorary chairman. The council was a success almost from the start. Most importantly, it was rooted in the parishes of the neighborhood. In time, the council sponsored food, health and recreational programs. Eventually it forced the local Democratic organization to recognize it as a legitimate and permanent organization.

⌐ Back of the Yards brought Alinsky nationwide acclaim. In 1946 he codified his technique of organizing in *Reveille For Radicals*, a passionately upbeat manifesto that outlined how all neighborhoods could transform themselves through democratically run "People's Organizations," just like the council. Alinsky wrote: "The kind of participation that comes out of a People's Organization. . . .completely changes what had previously been to John Smith, assembly-line American, a dull, gray monotonous road of existence that stretched out interminably, into a brilliantly lit, highly exciting avenue of hope, drama, conflict, with, at the end of the street the most brilliant ending known to the mind of man — the future of mankind."

Of course, Alinsky continued, the people cannot reach this future alone. They need an organizer, a behind-the-scenes strategist who knows the community, discovers its "native" leaders and then simplifies, personifies and dramatizes its thorny problems, while never hesitating when necessary to stir the embers of discontent.

"The organizer dedicated to changing the life of a particular community must first rub raw the resentment of the people. . . . fan the latent hostilities of many of the people to the point of overt expression. He must search out controversy and issues, rather than avoid them," he wrote in *Reveille For Radicals*, adding in *Rules For Radicals*, published in 1971: "It is essential that [issues] be simple enough to be grasped as rallying or battle cries. They can not be generalities like sin or immorality or the good life or morals. They must be this immorality of this slum landlord with this slum tenement where these people suffer."

In the end, it was this aggressive endorsement of confrontation tactics for which Alinsky is most remembered. He loved to devise outrageous schemes (such as his threatened "fart-in," in which hundreds of protesters would eat baked beans and then attend a concert). The purpose of such acts was to torment the powerful, while rallying his supporters and drawing attention to their cause. "Saul was a funny and irreverent man," says Monsignor John Egan, a close Alinsky friend and ally from many projects in racially changing areas on Chicago's southwest and northwest sides. "Saul never took himself seriously. But, my God, he took the problems and the people seriously."

In many ways, Alinsky was emulating his hero, John L. Lewis. The parameters for action, both men agreed, must be flexible for people in desperate times. "The biggest job of a leader is to develop a rationale, a moral basis for these spontaneous actions," Alinsky told *Harper's*. "When the first sit-down [auto worker] strikes took place, no one had really planned them. They were clearly a violation of the law. . . . But Lewis issued a pontifical statement: 'A man's right to a job transcends the right of private property.' It undergirded the situation with a purpose, a direction. If [Lewis] had not done this, the strikes might well have collapsed."

"Tactics of confrontation were necessary in Chicago because otherwise the political organization would not respond," says Josh Hoyt, who has organized for UNO. "The community organizations were like governments in exile. They had so little power. Their only strength was in numbers, and they had to fight for everything they got."

Alinsky never intended for such tactics to be ends in and of themselves. The hard work was rooting a group in its neighborhood. But over time, Alinsky's tactics obscured his organizations' accomplishments. All too often, critics charged, Alinsky groups gave little attention to the value or worth of their goals and fell into the habit of confrontation for its own sake.

Such was the case in the 1970s when several groups, including the Northwest Community Organization, pressed school officials to do away with the traditional hour-long lunch break. The residents contended that their children, walking to and from school, were vulnerable to attack by gangs. Many teachers countered that it was educationally unsound and stifling to confine children in a classroom for five-and-a-half hours with only a 20-minute break. The parents persisted, accentuating their protests with promises to devise creative solutions to any problems emerging from the shorter school day.

In the end, most schools capitulated, after which the parents' enthusiasm waned. No solutions were created, and eventually most of the organizers who had led the protests, found other jobs and left the community.

"Organizing in poor communities is never a smooth and easy process," says Sheila Radford Hill, a veteran organizer for the Chicago Area Project — a citywide group founded by Alinsky's early associate, Clifford Shaw, to combat juvenile delinquency. "Often you have to set reachable goals and settle for smaller victories along the way."

In general, Alinsky-style groups have had only short-lived success in poor communities where there are few stable church or civic groups to hook into. An even greater failure has been their inability to coalesce groups from different neighborhoods. Part of the problem stems from existing turf squabbles and rivalries. But tensions often are fostered when organizations compete for grants, newspaper headlines and even members. "Sometimes there's a tendency to get into competitive matches," says Shel Trapp, who together with Gale Cincotta organized National People's Action, a network of community organizations based in Chicago. "All too often, Alinsky-style groups get too parochial."

The problem is fiercest in changing neighborhoods when whites, for instance, resist blacks, or Mexicans ostracize Puerto Ricans. Indeed, one of Chicago's strongest organizations — UNO, Back of the Yards — emerged precisely because Hispanics and blacks felt locked out of existing organizations. Alinsky described the process as a struggle between the "Have-Not's" and the "Have-a-Little-and-Want-More's."

"Too often I've seen the have-nots turn into haves and become just as crummy as the haves they used to envy," Alinsky told *Harper's*. "Some of the fruit ranchers in California steam around in Cadillacs and treat the Mexican-American field hands like vermin. Know who those bastards are? They're the characters who rode west in Steinbeck's trucks in *The Grapes of Wrath*."

And then there is the question of bigotry. "I can not say that an Alinsky group has ever organized black and white communities into one," says the Rev. Arthur Brazier, founding president of The Woodlawn Organization and pastor of the Apostolate Church of God on the city's south side. "People don't organize for the sake of organizing. They organize around specific purposes. And I haven't seen any efforts along those lines."

That may be an understatement. For when it came to racial hostilities, Alinsky by his own admission was almost helpless. He condemned bigotry, yes. And he supported the concept of integration. One of his most noble, ambitious endeavors, the Greater Southwest Side Organization, even attempted during the late 1960s and early 1970s to stem the massive resegregation of several neighborhoods just west of the city's Dan Ryan Expressway.

But Alinsky dismissed as naive any effort to organize against racism. "Look at a community like Cicero, Illinois," he said in the *Harper's* interview. "You don't start out right off the bat by saying, 'Racists are banned from this organization, and we're going to fight for the right to bring blacks in here.' If you do that, they'll all walk out on you and you'll have nobody to communicate with. So you avoid the race issue. You leave it alone. You know that once you have them organized on other issues, the situation will change."

And so it was that Alinsky or his disciples organized groups in black or white communities, but could never unite these organizations as one. If blacks and whites came together over a cause of common concern — as they did in the early 1970s with opposition to the Crosstown Expressway, a massive project proposed by Mayor Richard J. Daley that would have obliterated several communities — the union crumbled after the issue disappeared. And all too quickly hatred and animosity bubbled to the surface, as in the mayoral election of 1983. Even Alinsky, toward the end of his life, acknowledged that bigotry limited his effectiveness as an organizer, particularly among blacks.

"All kinds of walls are up now, which in some ways are as bad as the old segregationist walls," Alinsky said in *Harper's*. "Right now you have blacks saying, 'Whitey get lost.' So, I accept that fact that today, in spite of my record, my white skin disqualifies me from the kind of direct organizing work I've done in Chicago and Rochester [New York] and other ghettos. In this climate, I'm convinced that all whites should get out of the black ghettos. It's a stage we have to go through."

Not surprisingly, by the end of the 1960s, Alinsky pledged to turn his attention to the plight of the white middle class. "Suppose you could get all the blacks, Mexican-Americans, poor whites and Puerto Ricans organized,"

Alinsky said in *Harper's*. "That would be maybe 55 million people by the end of the 1970s. But the population will be around 225 million by then, so the poor will still be a minority who need allies, and they'll have to find supporters among the three-quarters of our people who are middle class. . . . In some ways, the middle-class groups are more alienated than even the poor. There aren't any special funding programs for them. They don't have any special admissions to universities. They don't have a special anything, except getting constantly clobbered by taxes and inflation. These people are just thrashing around in their own frustrations."

Today, many organizers wrestle with the same dilemmas. Some, like Trapp and Cincotta, have made impressive strides. In 1976, their group, National People's Action, lobbied locally and nationally and forced Congress to pass the Community Reinvestment Act. The law, condemned by many bankers as blackmail, compels banks to set aside a portion of their holdings for inner-city mortgages and business loans. Last September, the law enabled the Greater Roseland Coalition for Community Control to force a nearby bank to guarantee $20 million in loans for their working-class black, south-side neighborhood.

Other activists, like Heather Booth, have attempted to wed Alinsky's grass-roots activism with the sophisticated mass-marketing techniques of corporate America. A former civil rights activist, Booth never trained under Alinksy, but she has read his books. Booth settled in Chicago in the late 1960s and formed the Midwest Academy, a training school for organizers, and Citizen Action, a nationwide coalition of groups whose interests range from foreign policy to utilities. Citizen Action organizers go door to door in communities across the country, putting together mailing lists and phone banks that can be tapped for elections or congressional hearings, like the 1987 hearings over Robert Bork's nomination to the U.S. Supreme Court.

"There are limitations to parochial Alinsky organizing, particularly when our lives are affected by decisions made on a national or international level. Whether we send our children to fight in Central America is just as important to most people on Main Street as a toxic plant in the backyard," says Booth. "We also have to take into consideration demographic trends. There are more families with two working parents. How do you reach them? You need new approaches, you have to take advantage of new technologies. It isn't that we're doing away with Alinsky's tactics. I think of it as growth."

Chambers, too, has altered his mentor's teachings. After Alinsky died, Chambers moved the Industrial Areas Foundation from Chicago to New York, in part, to assist a chapter there that was struggling. "Saul wasn't perfect, but we learn from our mistakes," says Chambers. "For one thing we stay with our groups. Saul used to organize them and leave them alone. We didn't have the resources to stick with them, and we also hoped that after a few years they would exist as independent self-sufficient entities. But, you know what happens. Leadership changes. Have-nots become haves. Some organizers don't want to leave, and they turn the group into their own little power base."

Chambers also updated many of Alinsky's precepts: "We're rotating organizers now. We've moved guys from New York to Minnesota. That keeps them fresh, keeps them from burning out. And another thing, we pay them more. They make as much as $50,000. No more of the days when you worked for free and wore a hair shirt. This should be a career job. I'm the oldest at 56, and there's a big group of organizers in their 40s."

But some fundamentals have not changed since the early days in the Back of the Yards. To succeed, an organization must be firmly rooted in its community. "We only go to communities that want us," Chambers says. "They have to invite us. And we say, 'Fine, you want us? Here's the bill.' They have to finance us themselves through dues. We don't take foundation money. Foundations only give you money with strings attached. Sure, it works in poor communities. They've got money for cigarettes, candy and alcohol, don't they? Well, they can pay dues too. I'm in Baltimore now, celebrating the anniversary of Build. It's based in a poor black community, and it's 10 years old and going strong. So, you see, we're fighting. We're making progress. We're learning. The struggle hasn't gone away."

UNO:
Organizing at the Grass Roots

by Wilfredo Cruz

'UNO is about empowering people to organize themselves so people can have decisionmaking power over the decisions that will affect them, their communities and their families.'
Danny Solis

I n Chicago's southeast side neighborhood stands the modern $3.5 million Ninos Heroes Magnet Public Elementary School built in 1981. Nearby is the City of Chicago's $1.3 million public health clinic renovated in March 1983. In November 1986 Gov. James R. Thompson restored $23.7 million in state funds to Chicago for construction of eight public elementary schools in largely Hispanic neighborhoods. Five are under construction; work is to begin this year on the remaining three. Probably none of this would have come about without the efforts of the United Neighborhood Organization (UNO). Its members — mainly poor and working-class Mexican-Americans — pushed, fought and pressured city and state officials to build the school, renovate the clinic and restore the funds.

UNO has earned a reputation as a strong advocacy organization, applying the principles of the late Saul Alinsky to build church-based, grass-roots organizations in diverse Mexican-American neighborhoods across the city. "UNO's doing some of the best church-based community organizing in Chicago. They have a good track record of accomplishments. And they involve a lot of people in their organizing," says Jackie Kendall, director of Chicago's Midwest Academy, a national center for training organizers and building progressive coalitions.

Founded in 1980, UNO has affiliated chapters in four lower-income, largely Mexican-American neighborhoods. There's an UNO chapter in southeast Chicago near the Indiana border. Once a stable, working-class neighborhood, it was hammered hard in the 1980s by an economic recession that shuttered steel mills. Just southwest of the Loop, UNO thrives in Pilsen, one of the oldest communities in Chicago. A port of entry for Mexican immigrants, Pilsen's 150-year-old buildings sag under the

Formerly a reporter for *The Chicago Reporter*, Wilfredo Cruz is director of public information at the Chicago Public Library. He has a Ph.D. in Social Service Administration from the University of Chicago. The United Neighborhood Organization (UNO) was the subject of his dissertation. "UNO: Organizing at the Grass Roots" was first published in the April 1988 *Illinois Issues*.

weight of a steady influx of new arrivals. West of Pilsen, UNO operates in Little Village, a neighborhood of modest two-flats and bungalows, which is fast becoming another port of entry. And finally, UNO organizes in the Back of the Yards, once thriving stockyard country. Community organizing began here in 1939 when Alinsky put together his famous neighborhood council, a coalition of Irish, Poles and Lithuanians, many of whom left as Mexican-Americans moved in.

Together, UNO groups claim over 1,000 members and several thousand supporters, mainly parishioners from 20 Catholic city parishes. "I think what really gives our organization strength is the parishes. Without parishes, you really don't have an organization," says Salvador Roman, an UNO leader and president of UNO of Little Village.

Like Alinsky, UNO's organizers challenge their members not to be the passive objects of other people's decisions. Organizers teach Mexican-Americans how to wield their organizational people power. "UNO is about empowering people to organize themselves so people can have decisionmaking power over the decisions that will affect them, their communities and their families," explains Danny Solis, executive director of UNO of Chicago, located in Pilsen and headquarters for the other four UNO groups. "Right now that power doesn't exist in minority communities, let alone the Hispanic community."

UNO members feel that by banding together they can gain the power to tackle problems and improve their neighborhoods. The Rev. George Schoop, pastor of St. Kelvin's parish in southeast Chicago says: "UNO represents hope to this neighborhood. And over the years UNO has delivered on many of the hopes of the people. Some health care, some employment training classes at Olive Harvey College, some better city services, voter registration and a limitation on toxic dumping were won by this neighborhood because of UNO's organizing."

UNO was founded by Mary Gonzales and her husband Gregory Galluzzo, two experienced community organizers. Gonzales heard about Communities Organized for Public Service (COPS), a church-based organization in San Antonio, Texas. Established by the Alinsky-founded Industrial Areas Foundation in the early 1970s and still in existence today, COPS was empowering Mexican-Americans and winning millions of dollars in neighborhood improvements. Gonzales felt that a group like COPS but with citywide impact was needed for Chicago's Mexican-Americans, who lacked power and were often short-changed of crucial city services. Indeed, in 1980 when the first UNO chapter came into being, the number of Mexican-Americans in the Chicago area had more than tripled since 1970, increasing from 93,389 to 310,428. Nearly half of those over 18 years old had no more than an eighth grade education, and most Mexican-Americans worked in low-skilled jobs, with a per capita income of about $5,000.

The Latino Institute, a social service agency in downtown Chicago —

criticized by some Hispanics for not providing more of its resources to inner-city Hispanic neighborhoods — sponsored Gonzales for several years as she created the UNO network. Gonzales and Galluzzo convinced several parishes in southeast Chicago to form the first UNO chapter. Funds were quickly raised. "Foundations had neglected Latinos, so they poured money into UNO of southeast Chicago. Within two years we had a budget of about $160,000," recalls Galluzzo. By the end of 1983, UNO of Little Village and UNO of Back of the Yards were similarly formed; the fourth chapter, Pilsen Neighbors Community Council, an already established advocacy group, also joined the network.

Annual budgets of the nonprofit UNO groups range from $72,000 to $280,000. Parishes contribute from $2,000-5,000 yearly; fundraising and small grants from Chicago philanthropies account for the rest. Gonzales now serves as associate director of UNO of Chicago, and former UNO director Galluzzo heads the Gamaliel Foundation, which trains organizers and gives technical assistance to Chicago and downstate community organizations like the Quad Cities Interfaith Organizing Committee.

In typical Alinsky fashion UNO groups avoid taking on unwinnable issues to prevent defeatism among their members. For example, Wisconsin Steel in southeast Chicago shut down late in 1980, throwing about 3,500 people out of work. UNO knew it couldn't do anything to reopen the mill, so it didn't try.

But emphasis on winnable issues leads some to question UNO's effectiveness. "UNO's orientation to organizing is pretty conservative. They concentrate almost entirely on safe, bread-and-butter issues, like putting in a stop sign, garbage pickup, that sort of thing. They don't take up citywide or larger political issues affecting Hispanics," says Roberto Rey, a former organizer for UNO and Comite Latino. The latter is an Uptown-based, Alinsky-style group organizing South and Central American Hispanics on local issues like tenant rights, immigration and naturalization, and hiring of more Hispanics in the Chicago Park District. Two years ago Comite Latino invited Ernesto Cardenal, "poet of the Nicaraguan revolution," to Chicago to speak to its members. That led to counter protest by Chicago's anti-communist Cubans and underscores the difficulty of organizing the city's uniquely diverse Hispanic community.

In response to critics, UNO's staff explains that while stop signs and better garbage pickups may seem like small issues to others, they're significant to neighborhood residents. They also contend that political ideological issues such as Nicaragua's revolution are irrelevant and divisive to Chicago's Hispanics, who already have plenty of socioeconomic problems to deal with.

Moreover, UNO doesn't claim to represent all Hispanics. It says it speaks for about 5 percent of the city's Mexican-Americans. In 1985 UNO did try to organize Puerto Ricans and form another parish-based UNO chapter in the Puerto Rican neighborhoods of West Town and Humboldt

Park on the city's near north side. But Puerto Rican leaders vehemently complained that UNO was an outsider. "We don't go into their neighborhoods organizing their people, why should they come into ours? That's a lack of respect," the Rev. Jorge Morales, a Puerto Rican leader, said at the time. Morales is cofounder of the West Town Concerned Citizens Coalition, a once active Alinsky-style group. Parishes in the area quickly shied away from UNO, forcing it to pull out. The incident clearly shows the parochialism of Alinsky-style groups, which refuse to cooperate with one another while zealously competing for turf, recognition, members and funds.

But in spite of rivalries with other groups and the persistence of urban problems which extend far beyond neighborhood boundaries, UNO has been able to slow down the deterioration of inner-city neighborhoods, improve existing services and generate new ones. Equally important, UNO helps residents acquire a voice in the renewal of their neighborhoods, as they pressure public officials to be accountable to their needs. Theresa Fragra, an outspoken UNO leader and former president of UNO of Pilsen says: "We want the superintendent of public schools, the mayor and politicians to listen to us, treat us as equals and include our needs and issues in their agendas. We want to be respected and not have to go to the superintendent's house at night to give him a message from the community."

Influential public officials are regularly invited to UNO's neighborhood meetings to hear the community's messages and demands on specific issues. To ensure maximum turnout, UNO groups rent school buses and arrange babysitting services for their predominately female members. Anywhere from 300 to 3,500 people attend these meetings, applauding loudly when public officials concede to their demands or booing wildly when they do not. If meetings fail to win issues, UNO members intensify the confrontation tactics — demonstrating and picketing at the offices and homes of public officials and holding sit-ins, call-ins, etc. — to press their case.

Some community residents refuse to join UNO, frowning at its aggressive methods. "Second and third generation Mexican-Americans are very Americanized and think they are part of the system and have won their piece of the pie. They feel you don't go around doing those kinds of things," says Gonzales.

Lately, UNO is using more negotiation and lobbying and less confrontation. Some wonder if UNO is losing its toughness. Last year, for example, UNO's negotiations failed to persuade Chicago immigration officials to place an immigration and legalization office in Pilsen; three offices were placed in non-Mexican areas of Chicago. Some of UNO's members in Pilsen and Little Village wanted to apply for American citizenship through the federal government's new immigration amnesty program. Mike Royko, syndicated columnist for the *Chicago Tribune*, took the wind out of UNO's sails, writing that Mexicans could easily pay 95 cents to jump on a bus and travel to the other immigration offices. "Royko missed the point," says Kelvin Jackson, an UNO organizer: "About 77 percent of the people who are applying for amnesty come from the Mexican community. Why can't this community have an office? The point was, we didn't want to be ignored."

But UNO's organizers deny they're losing punch. Toned-down tactics show they're gaining respect from the system, they argue. The late Mayor Harold Washington did seem to respect UNO, and UNO rarely employed

---

Mary Gonzales: 'You can't sit back and do nothing

Saul Alinsky staunchly believed women could not be good community organizers. Women lacked toughness, street-smarts and astuteness, he felt. But had Alinsky met Mary Gonzales of the United Neighborhood Organization (UNO), he'd quickly change his mind. Gonzales is considered the best and most dynamic organizer in Chicago. According to veteran organizer Peter Martinez, who worked closely with Alinsky and has trained UNO organizers: "Gonzales is a good strategist. She's got what it takes to win issues. Her ability as trainer and developer of leadership among people is outstanding."

Tall, with a commanding presence, Gonzales, 47, has been organizing in Chicago's predominately Mexican-American neighborhoods for about 17 years. She was the mastermind in the creation of UNO and is currently its lead organizer and associate director. She has also worked with community groups like Pilsen Neighbors Community Council and The Latino Institute.

Throughout her career, Gonzales has helped Mexican-Americans, blacks and whites win improvements in the areas of health, education, housing, city services, transportation and job training. She has also trained and mentored hundreds of lay leaders, who respect her and see her as a role model. She says: "An organizer's job is to challenge people to take a stand and act on things they see as valuable — family, church, community. You can't say 'I believe in this' and sit back and do nothing. You've got to act to improve those things and challenge institutions to live up to those values."

Many city and state public officials know Gonzales as the keen strategist bringing hundreds of community residents to their front doors demanding that they take action on neighborhood issues. While Gonzales is glad more Hispanics and blacks are winning elected office, she warns: "I don't care if you're an Hispanic, black or white politician, you've got to be accountable to the people you serve."

"If I had a problem in my neighborhood, I would want Mary Gonzales organizing my neighbors to get it resolved. She's that good. She's intelligent,

abrasive tactics against him. Washington attended many UNO meetings and backed many of its issues, including twice-a-week garbage pickup for Pilsen in 1983, a $1.3 million City Colleges of Chicago job training center in south Chicago in 1985, and moratoriums on new waste landfills in southeast Chicago that expire in February 1989. When Mary Montes, an UNO leader and current president of UNO of Southeast Chicago, aggressively questioned the major on landfills at a public meeting, Washington admiringly said: "Boy, you're a tough woman. I don't want to mess with you. I'll do anything you want me to do." Shortly before

---

hard-working, sophisticated, and she's not self-righteous," says Eduardo Camacho, who has consulted with over 100 community organizations as research director of the Community Renewal Society.

Gonzales is an anomaly in organizing circles. Most organizers are white, male and college-educated. They usually don't live in the neighborhoods they organize, and they tend to leave organizing after several years. But Gonzales is Mexican-American, a high-school graduate, a longtime resident of Pilsen, and a career organizer. A mother of four — two daughters in college, one in high school and a son in kindergarten — Gonzales got her first taste of community activism in the late 1950s when she tagged along to meetings with her mother, Guadalupe Reyes. An active volunteer in Pilsen's settlement houses and social service agencies, Reyes founded the Esperanza School for mentally handicapped children in 1972. From these experiences, Gonzales learned that residents are willing to work collectively to improve their neighborhoods. When she was in her teens — and, she says, a wallflower — she got involved in bettering neighborhood social services.

In 1971 Gonzales and Gregory Galluzzo, a former Jesuit priest, worked together at Pilsen Neighbors Community Council. They married in 1979. Gonzales credits Galluzzo with helping her realize that many problems of Pilsen residents couldn't be solved by social services alone and that organizing and advocacy were necessary. During the 1970s Gonzales and Galluzzo moved the council from social services into advocacy. They won numerous tenant issues, organized parent groups and forced Chicago Board of Education officials to build Benito Juarez High School in Pilsen in 1977.

"You might want to take this with a grain of salt because I'm her husband, but Mary is a winner. People are attracted to her because she is a winner. She's not afraid of telling it like it is. She's willing to face bureaucrats or anyone else and kick their ass if she has to. She's a heroine in her community," says Galluzzo.

---

his death, he appointed Montes to the Chicago City Colleges Board of Trustees.

UNO continues using negotiation to cultivate support among Chicago's changing political players. Politicians are invited to UNO's accountability night forums in parish halls, and they often back UNO's issues. In return, members usually vote for these politicians. But UNO carefully avoids close friendship with politicians, fearing that it might be taken for granted.

Recently, these tactics paid off. For the last three years UNO groups, concerned about rising unemployment, tried to convince City Colleges of Chicago to build a state-of-the-art facility to train residents for future technical jobs. UNO lobbied key politicians such as Mayor Washington, state legislators and local Hispanic aldermen. In November 1987, Salvatore Rotella, chancellor of City Colleges of Chicago, announced that construction would soon begin on a $40 million West Side Technical Institute to be located at 27th and South Western, bordering the Pilsen and Little Village neighborhoods.

Sometimes UNO gets angry enough to resort to its old confrontation tactics. In February 1988, for example, 100 UNO members protested a plan by Waste Management Inc. to spend millions of dollars on community development projects in southeast Chicago. The company proposed to invest the money to win neighborhood cooperation for its continued waste disposal in the area after the 1989 moratorium expires. But UNO members argue that southeast Chicago is already highly polluted with the company's toxic waste dumps. Shouting "No deals!" they marched to a local bank and broke into a meeting being conducted by James Fitch, president of South Chicago Bank, who was leading community discussion of the plan. "We will fight you every step of the way," Montes, quoted in the Chicago *Sun-Times*, told the astonished Fitch and other residents at the meeting. The plan is stalled. Montes promises that UNO will continue to oppose the plan and the opening of new Waste Management dumps in the area.

Like Alinsky in his organizing days, UNO sees parishes as institutions that can facilitate neighborhood organizing. Parishes provide UNO groups with a sense of legitimacy, funds, free meeting rooms and offices, and most important of all, a large supply of potential supporters, members and lay leaders. "Heck, if our church backs them on an issue, UNO knows they got people there. By golly, we can produce a couple hundred people. So it became clear to UNO that if you want the numbers, the churches are the place to get them. If we decide to do it, it will be done," says the Rev. Gerard Cleator, pastor of St. Pias Church in Pilsen.

Some priests join UNO out of religious conviction to help the disadvantaged. But priests also join because UNO's organizers spend a lot of time helping them and their laity to improve their parishes. Ironically, while Chicago's Mexican-American population is booming, only about a dozen of the city's 1,000 diocesan parish priests are Hispanic. Thus white priests look to UNO for help. Organizers work with priests and laity to increase parish membership and Sunday collections, improve fundraising, increase parish school enrollment and plan Spanish and English religious services, retreats and parish outreach.

But UNO's relationship with parishes is not all heavenly. Organizers express disappointment that while priests are generally pleased with UNO's assistance to parishes, some priests are not encouraging their parishioners to actively participate in UNO's neighborhood advocacy efforts. "We found that there are real limitations to what you can do with the church. The basic reason is because you've got a lot of white priests whose fundamental self-interests are advancing within the church hierarchy and not making life better for their constituency," says Josh Hoyt, a former UNO organizer.

One UNO organizer, who requested anonymity, thinks priests shun UNO because higher church officials see it as a threat. He recalls that a parish priest was told by Joseph Cardinal Bernardin "that while he liked the work UNO was doing with parishes, he hoped they didn't try to form a separate church."

Two parishes ended their participation in UNO of Little Village because priests and some parishioners didn't feel it was the church's responsibility to engage in neighborhood advocacy. Three other parishes in Pilsen — possibly fearing resistance from higher church officials — decided to distance their ties with UNO. According to Father Cleator, "It became a conflict of who is really running the church. UNO was so involved in helping to organize the parishes, sensing that it was a most important institution. But then the question became: Who are we accountable to, UNO or the Archdiocese?"

Monsignor John J. Egan, a close friend of Alinsky, laments that churches are not more involved with groups like UNO. Egan recalls that the early 1960s, a time of civic crisis, was the "golden age" of church cooperation with Alinsky-style groups in Chicago. Egan challenges the church to continue this legacy: "I personally don't think the Catholic Church is giving that much support to Latino organizations in Chicago. There should be far more support so the organizations can get stronger and stronger," says Egan. "After all, Latino groups come into our city and they have been exploited, pushed around; they have problems of unemployment, dropouts. And for us, Hispanic people are a great treasure; they're part of a whole Roman Catholic tradition. We should put money, personnel and all the resources we have, to enable them to acquire the fulfillment of their dreams. They're our people."

Like UNO, other groups have had difficulty integrating churches with community organizing. In 1985 several organizers failed to form a new Alinsky-style group in West Town and Humboldt Park by organizing storefront Pentecostal churches. Peter Earle, one of the organizers, explains that Hispanic reverends in Pentecostal churches are conservative. They believe the poor shall realize justice in heaven and shouldn't get involved in worldly matters, Earle says. He also believes that they like to maintain control over their congregations and fear organizers might steal their flocks.

UNO continues working with parishes, hoping church officials will eventually heed Egan's words. But UNO is also diversifying. Currently it is organizing parent groups in public elementary schools and working with local social service agencies on a planning grant to upgrade the Pilsen business district. On the education front UNO's parent groups recently won hot-lunch programs, building repair and upgrading, the right to form parent groups and better principal-teacher-parent communication at public schools in Pilsen, Little Village and Back of the Yards. UNO contends that Chicago school officials are not adequately addressing problems in Mexican-American schools. "As far as we can see, our schools are getting less attention than black schools. I'm talking about overcrowding and a lack of programs, discipline, maintenance and security. [Former School Supt.] Ruth Love may have been more political, but at least she paid attention to us," Danny Solis said in a February 1987 *Chicago Magazine* article on Manford Byrd Jr., Chicago's current school superintendent. UNO's plan for school reform calls for more parental involvement in local schools, decentralization and a limit on class size. (See "The Chicago School Mess" in the April 1988 *Illinois Issues.*)

One of UNO's overlooked achievements is its ongoing development of leadership among its members. UNO's organizer mentoring and leadership sessions have produced about 30 leaders who lead others on issues and articulate UNO's concerns in large public meetings and closed door negotiating sessions. There are also about 300 leaders who do the support work necessary for effective organizing: phoning people to get them to meetings, distributing flyers, arranging media coverage and serving on committees and fund-raising drives. Many leaders say that through UNO they have gained the personal growth and self-confidence needed to improve their lives. Some are entering college, studying for G.E.D.s, taking English classes and becoming American citizens.

Southeast Chicago's Montes explains: "I've learned to negotiate a lot better, to think more strategically. I've learned to deal with people who, at one time, I was afraid to deal with. Like Governor James Thompson — he's no big deal anymore. He's a person just like me. I've learned to work in collaboration with others." Graciela Schuch, an UNO leader and former president of UNO Back of the Yards adds: "UNO's organizers teach us how to run meetings, how to develop strategies, what to look for in a problem. They kind of push you to look for solutions. To me, it has been a tremendous experience. It has enriched my life."

It's not certain what UNO's future holds. It has survived the "five-year-blues," the time most community organizations fall apart. And foundations steadily funnel funds to UNO. Yet in the past some Alinsky-style groups that appeared to be growing have been crippled or broken by problems that suddenly surfaced. For example, as UNO takes on larger, time-consuming issues like the Technical Institute, smaller issues and leadership training at the local chapters tend to be ignored, causing disillusionment among members. "I think UNO has to get its grass roots strengthened. It's not as strong right now as it was. There's the danger of wheeling and dealing on the high political level and forgetting some of the grass roots," says Father Cleator.

UNO's decisionmaking is increasingly top to bottom, with organizers and experienced staff making many major decisions. Limited decisionmaking hurts morale. This seems to have happened to The Woodlawn Organization (TWO), a black, Alinsky-style group founded in 1961 in Chicago's Woodlawn neighborhood. For the last couple of years TWO has been experiencing internal dissension about administrative decisionmaking and the future of the organization.

In later years groups like UNO have tended to move away from advocacy into social services, and they sometimes mismanage these programs. This happened to the West Town Concerned Citizens Coalition, which was a strong advocacy group during the late 1970s. Today the coalition tries to survive as a quiet, small social service group. Its $1 million housing rehabilitation program was severely mismanaged, and it folded in 1982.

UNO's staff agrees that keeping an organization together, organizing daily and winning issues is extremely difficult. But they're confident they can learn from the mistakes of other groups. For the future, UNO will aim to strengthen its organization by developing Hispanic organizers, encouraging more men to join the local chapters and training many more leaders at the grass-roots level. Ultimately, UNO is confident that new ideas and new members will continue to come from the grass roots, invigorating the organization and maintaining it as a vehicle for the empowerment of community residents.

.

SON/SOC: Organizing in White Ethnic Neighborhoods

by Paul M. Green

*'We must stop being made to feel ashamed
or apologetic about being who we are.'*
SON/SOC

L egendary community organizer Saul Alinsky wrote in his 1971
book, *Rules for Radicals*: "Change comes from power. . . . and
power comes from organization." For Alinksy, "Power is the
reason for being of organizations." He did not limit his analysis only to
society's so-called "have-nots." He also wrote about the "have-a-little-
want-mores." These individuals are working-class to lower-middle-class
people whom Alinsky believes are "torn between upholding the status quo
to protect the little they have — yet, wanting change so *they can get more.*"

Historically, Chicago has been home to countless thousands of "have-
a-little-want-mores." They are the blue-collar workers who live in the
neighborhoods and parishes, work in the factories and small businesses
and dream about a better life for themselves and their children. To
improve their lot they have joined unions, become active in local politics
and formed neighborhood improvement associations. Key to their dreams
is neighborhood stability. Their upward mobility hinges on whether the
value of their small homes increases or at least remains the same. Why? If
things work out, they or their children can sell the home and move to a
better neighborhood, a bigger house, a brighter future. Or, if their
ambitions are not fulfilled, they can at least live out their lives in the
dignity and safety of the old neighborhood.

Today individuals who fit Alinsky's description of "have-a-little-want-
mores" reside on Chicago's northwest and southwest sides. Mainly white
ethnic (though there is a growing mix of blacks and Hispanics on the
southwest side), these city dwellers face demographic, political and
economic changes that seem to be closing out their options. In response,
they have formed a network of Alinsky-style community organizations.
They have used the church as a key organizational tool. They have selected

Paul M. Green is director of the Institute for Public Policy and Administration, Governors State University. A columnist and political commentator,
his most recent books include *Paul Green's Chicago* and *Bashing Chicago
Traditions: Harold Washington's Last Campaign*, coauthored with Melvin G.
Holli. "SON/SOC: Organizing in White Ethnic Communities" first
appeared in the May 1988 *Illinois Issues.*

issues that are admittedly in their self-interest to generate community support and they have attempted to negotiate with governmental entities to reach compromise solutions. They call themselves The Save-Our-Neighborhoods/Save Our City (SON/SOC) coalition. Funded mainly through individual contributions with some support from foundations, SON/SOC is an umbrella structure for community and church groups that make up the Northwest Neighborhood Federation and the Southwest Parish and Neighborhood Federation.

"Everybody has the right to obtain power," says Mike Smith, a burly and gregarious professional organizer. He and SON/SOC's other full-time organizer, Bob Gannett, believe that their group has operated totally and purely within the "true Alinsky model." Gannett says, "We are independent politically and economically. . . . our people do not get paid or go into politics. . . ." Indeed, SON/SOC's neighborhood organizations should earn high praise from Chicago's populist-progressive organizers and community groups. And they once did. But that ended with Harold Washington's 1983 mayoral victory and the continuing dominance of race in Chicago politics and thinking. Today SON/SOC is outside of the close-knit cadre of community groups that influences the liberal political and socioeconomic scene in the city. Gannett says, "We do not get respect [because] individuals and institutions are unable to go beyond stereotypes." Why?

Basically SON/SOC is a white ethnic organization trying to deal with the race problem in Chicago *at the neighborhood level.* And as Gannett and Smith point out, SON/SOC is sometimes at odds with both the left and the right on the political spectrum. Says Gannett, "Our leadership has stood up to four Chicago mayors, including Richard J. Daley, and thus we have never been favorites of the political establishment. They know they cannot control us." Who are these "SON/SOCkers" and where did they come from? The answer is a tale of two city neighborhoods: the southwest side and the northwest side.

The Southwest Parish and Neighborhood Federation (SPNF) began in 1971 when 12 people from two southwest side parishes (St. Gall and St. Nicolas of Tolentine) formed a community organization with the help of the Catholic Charities of Chicago. For several years individuals in these working-class Marquette Park neighborhoods had felt helpless to deal with the issues that were affecting their community. Dr. Martin Luther King Jr.'s march in 1966 followed by an invasion by some pro-Nazi groups had convinced residents that their area was being used as a convenient battleground to fight out a citywide race problem. It was clear that the direction of neighborhood change had placed their community on the racial frontier.

What is seldom discussed in analyzing racial change in Chicago and most northern cities is the chain of events that takes place. Converging on a neighborhood, unscrupulous real estate agents open storefront offices hoping to profit from the coming change. Often they encourage a speedy racial transition by panic peddling: frightening white homeowners to sell their homes below fair market prices, then reselling them at inflated prices to blacks. Banks become reluctant to lend money in the targeted neighborhood. Known as "redlining" because of the red lines drawn upon maps by financial institutions to designate neighborhoods considered poor investment risks, this discriminatory practice dries up mortgage and home improvement money.

SPNF fought redlining, first taking on a leading realtor and in 1974 challenging the community's financial giant, Talman Federal. The strategy was a "greenlining campaign" in which 10,000 local Talman savers signed petitions demanding that the bank reveal its lending data or else they would withdraw their savings. They won.

Two years later SPNF and Talman went head to head again. This time the community wanted Talman to fund a $15,000 study of two redevelopment proposals. One was for an "ethnic village," transforming 63rd Street into a culturally diverse specialty shop and restaurant district; the other proposed new moderate-income housing east of Western Avenue. When negotiations stalled, SPNF took action. On June 19, 1976, over 2,000 people marched on Talman carrying signs calling for "Redevelopment — not Violence." Long-time SPNF leader Jean Mayer, a toughminded woman who has lived on the southwest side with her family for over 29 years, still expresses amazement at the event. Many southwestsiders," explains Mayer, "called the bank St. Talman. . . . It was a god. . . . but the people were looking for a way to fight back." The protest caught the eye of Mayor Daley, who met later with march representatives, but his death that December ended all negotiations. "It's ironic," says Mayer, "when we took on Daley's City Hall or corporate America, the radical and liberal community organizers were in our corner. But later when we raised the same issues against Mayor Washington, they called us racists." Joe Cicero, who is executive director of the North River Commission on the northwest side, is anti-SON/SOC. He says, "What they're doing is organizing those who have bigotry in their hearts. It's as low as you can get as a community organizer." But Mayer and other SPNF leaders believe that they and their goals have not changed. She says, "We are and always have been average people who just want to protect our neighborhood."

Like their southwest side brethren, the Northwest Neighborhood Federation (NNF) began as a result of a small meeting. In June 1976 less than a dozen community activists met in the home of Dave and Carole Greason in Logan Square, an old neighborhood on the northwest side. Those attending were veterans of battles over redlining and the Crosstown Expressway. They were also members of the Citizens Action Program (CAP), a national, Alinsky-influenced, community organization network. At the meeting were Joe Crutchfield, former CAP treasurer, and Joyce Zick, chairperson of CAP's anti-Crosstown coalition. According to Gannett, "The origins of NNF stem from the experience of CAP and its successful fight to block the proposed Crosstown Expressway."

The Crosstown was the late Mayor Daley's dream. A 22-mile, billion-dollar expressway, it would have traversed Chicago north and south, linking up with other expressways and relieving traffic congestion downtown. Northwestsiders opposed to the Crosstown called it "Daley's ditch." Under the direction of CAP organizers, many of whom had been schooled in the ultraliberal Industrial Areas Foundation (IAF), an Alinsky training operation, community residents formed a coalition and stood up to the most powerful mayor in Chicago history. They argued that the Crosstown would destroy over 10,000 homes, displace over 30,000 people and eliminate over 1,800 jobs. They looked to the area churches for institutional support, and to some degree they found it. In the end, the Crosstown was defeated when state and city politicians cut a deal during the term of Mayor Jane Byrne.

That taste of what organized community power could accomplish was in the minds of those at the meeting in Logan Square. But so was another issue: their disillusionment with CAP and the IAF. According to Zick, "We were Chicagoans, interested mainly in our northwest side communities. . . . As CAP became more nationally oriented, they became less interested in our concerns." A feud had developed between CAP's IAF-trained professional organizers and the people in the northwest side neighborhoods. Arguments over funding and agenda priorities were turning allies into enemies. Zick says, "We had become the Afghanistan of the IAF, a client state."

In the months following the meeting a community organizing war broke out on the northwest side. The new Northwest Neighborhood Federation opened an office, hired Smith and Gannett as organizers and formulated long-range goals to establish its stability and credibility in the community. It eventually beat back a challenge from a new CAP/IAF-led organizing effort that tried to maintain the old structure on the northwest side. "Key to NNF's victory," in the words of Gannett, "was its ability to establish a people's agenda from the bottom up. The organization gave the people power and not the smoke and mirrors of CAP." For the next several years the fledgling organization worked on issues like redlining, housing and police protection.

In 1983 Harold Washington became Chicago's first black mayor. He swept into office riding the crest of a black political movement that advocated racial pride, economic fairness and a redistribution of power. Once again NNF and SPNF, after fighting City Hall for at least a decade, felt left out of the process. As the first year of Washington's term unfolded, both the mayor and his chief aldermanic foe Ald. Edward Vrdolyak played on racial fears as they hammered each other daily. SPNF and NNF activists bristled at administration charges that they had been pampered by previous Chicago mayors. They also challenged the stereotypical way some of the Chicago media viewed their communities and objected to the idea that their proposals were racist.

Frustrated by their new City Hall foes, fearful of their City Council champions — many of whom had opposed them in the Daley, Michael Bilandic and Byrne years —and frightened by their growing isolation in their own city, the northwest and southwest side community organizations decided to fight back by forming a Chicago-wide coalition called Save Our Neighborhoods/Save Our City.

SON/SOC was officially launched on February 1, 1984, when 150 NNF and SPNF members met at St. Turibius Church on the city's southwest side. They announced a first-of-its-kind white ethnic convention to be held April 29, the first anniversary of Mayor Washington's inauguration. Explaining the strategy, Mayer says: "This convention idea was to show the mayor that we could organize to defend our neighborhoods, tell him that we wanted to be part of the city and at the same time let him know that we were not 'sheet people' [supporters of the Ku Klux Klan]."

Launching its own newspaper just prior to the convention, SON/SOC reiterated its charges against Washington and at the same time called for reconciliation and understanding. The frustration and fears of a city dominated by the complicated issues of race, class and political competition were clearly visible in the paper's often scalding criticism of the mayor.

Most telling was an editorial affirming the right of white ethnics to determine their own identity: "We must stop being made to feel ashamed or apologetic about being who we are. For too long we have let others define 'white ethnic' as another name for racist. Who gives any leader, member of the press, educator or churchman — black, brown or white — the right to besmirch our good name, origins and accomplishments? This easy racist label must stop, or there will be no rational discussion left to be had in this town, just shouts and more name calling."

On April 29, 1984, over 1,000 SON/SOC delegates filled the grand ballroom of the Chicago Hyatt-Regency Hotel. Convention organizers produced 17,000 signed personal petitions from northwest and southwest side residents, who pledged their support and loyalty to SON/SOC's efforts. Keynote speaker Mayer centered most of her remarks on the theme of neighborhood stability — the same general topic she had first raised with other CAP leaders back in the anti-Crosstown Daley era. "We want to make sure the house we have sunk our money into won't lose its value through forces beyond our control. All we want is to hold onto something we have struggled so hard to achieve," she told the assembled delegates.

Press reaction to the convention was generally favorable. The most wanted response, however, came from Mayor Washington himself, who was attending a conference at Harvard University: "White ethnics have nothing to fear from my administration. . . . I will cooperate with all [their] worthy goals.

By autumn of 1984 peace had broken out between the mayor and SON/ SOC. A *Tribune* editorial called the new relationship "a strange, hopeful alliance." Key to the rapprochement were two prominent black Chicagoans. Insurance executive Alvin J. Robinson, a member of Chicago United (a liberal-oriented organization of some of the city's top business leaders that seeks to resolve racial tensions), used his longstanding friendship with Washington to bring about a quiet August summit meeting between the mayor and SON/SOC. Former 20th Ward Ald. Clifford Kelley added the political muscle of an elected official who for years had moved easily between the white and black communities in Chicago. A frequent guest on Chicago political commentator Bruce Dumont's popular WBEZ public radio program, "Inside Politics," Kelley was moved to action when he heard a SON/SOC member list his concerns about the mayor's attitude toward white ethnics. (It should be noted that Kelley was convicted of bribery in 1987 and is currently in a federal penitentiary. At the time of his sentencing, his friend and talk-show colleague Tom Roeser, a businessman and president of the City Club of Chicago, sent a character reference letter to the judge, highlighting Kelley's work on behalf of SON/ SOC and calling it "a mission for which he could derive no possible political or financial benefit.")

Washington now openly endorsed SON/SOC's Guaranteed Housing Equity Program (GHEP) and several other of its agenda items. The reconciliation reached its zenith in April 1985 when SON/SOC held a clout-heavy reception to present Robinson its "One Person Does Make a Difference Award." The high point of the evening was an appearance by the mayor. He charmed the crowd with his wit and excited their hopes with his calls for reconciliation. The racially mixed crowd cheered loudly as he concluded: "I intend to be. . . . one of the best mayors this city has ever had. I can only be that with your help."

What went wrong? Even up to the February 1987 mayoral primary, Washington continued to voice support for the coalition's home equity and linkage proposals — admittedly with some new reservations. However, his sweeping reelection victory gave him undisputed control of the City Council and ended the possibility of a white-ethnic threat to his leadership. Ever the shrewd pol, Washington recognized a new political reality based on his new political strength. If groups like SON/SOC had to be disappointed, so be it. White-ethnic Democratic politicians might give lip-service support to SON/SOC's agenda, but they were not going to go to the mat with Washington for an organization that had been a pain in the neck to them for over a decade.

Washington's opposition in the late fall of 1987 left SON/SOC with few vocal defenders. The mayor called SON/SOC people "zealots" and their proposals "divisive and confrontational." For veteran coalition members it was business as usual. They had been double-crossed by City

Hall and left once again to make their own way.

Beyond all the complicated issues and emotionally charged language is the dominant factor of race. The question facing SON/SOC today is a simple one: Can white ethnics organize to survive in a racially changing city without being labeled bigots? The debate rests on two points of view: historical racial reality v. futuristic racial idealism. SON/SOC members, many of them elderly homeowners, have seen one after another of their old working-class, bungalow communities racially integrated and then eventually resegregated. For those who attempted to stay, familiar streets turned strange and dangerous when economic decline followed racial turnover. Today most SON/SOC people find themselves with little room to maneuver in. They cannot afford to play racial "checkers" and jump over the problem by moving to the suburbs. Moreover, they are city people who have had a lifelong love affair with Chicago. As one elderly southwest side woman asked me, "Why should the burden of racial integration be placed solely on our shoulders?"

SON/SOC's agenda

Guaranteed Home Equity Program (GHEP): This plan would create a fund to guarantee property values in city neighborhoods voting to participate. Homeowners joining the program and keeping their property well-maintained for five years would have their homes guaranteed by the plan at 100 percent of current market value. GHEP would be funded by the property owners themselves through an annual fee based on each homeowner's Cook County tax assessment. Estimates of the fee range from $6 to $20 per year for five years. SON/SOC achieved a change in the state law in January 1987 to allow local advisory referenda in Chicago. GHEP was then presented to northwest and southwest side voters on April 7, 1987. It received 77,443 yes votes, an approval rating of over 90 percent. City and state ordinances proposed by SON/SOC to implement the GHEP on a "pilot" basis in these two areas are now awaiting legislative approval.

Linked development:. As part of the cost of developing Chicago's expanding downtown, lakefront and O'Hare areas, developers of major new office buildings would pay an "exaction" (a mandatory fee based on the size of the project) that would be used for neighborhood revitalization. Under the SON/SOC plan a neighborhood trust fund would be established to distribute linkage dollars equitably to the city's 77 neighborhood areas. Each area would then hold a local referendum to determine how its share should be spent. The proposal is awaiting action by the Chicago City Council.

FHA-VA lending policies; real estate abuses: Lax policies that allow unscrupulous mortgage bankers to fabricate false mortgage applications for

Yet if race seems to underlie all issues in Chicago, the city's changing population patterns show that class is replacing race as the new segregator of urban life. The growth areas surrounding the Loop, the expanding gentrified areas on the near northwest side and around DePaul University and Lakeview all have one thing in common: They are expensive. These "Yuppie-type" neighborhoods almost guarantee themselves a high percentage of white residents. And those blacks who can afford to join the gentrifying crowd will not be recent residents of the Chicago Housing Authority or working-class families with lots of school-age children. Like their white counterparts, black urban professionals are well-educated single persons or childless couples with a good deal of disposable income. In short, this is economic gerrymandering. As these upscale residents eliminate affordable housing by condo-ing and upgrading every building in sight, they put incredible pressure on city neighborhoods that still possess moderate and livable housing. Those are the neighborhoods that SON/SOC represents.

---

unqualified homeowners are a major SON/SOC concern. Many times when this happens, the new owner is unable to meet the payments; the mortgage is foreclosed; the house is boarded up; and the community suffers. SON/SOC has also been in the forefront of efforts to halt panic peddling and unwanted real estate solicitation and to ban "for sale" signs in city neighborhoods.

Crime: SON/SOC has always pushed for a fair distribution of police manpower for its neighborhoods. It also has pioneered in Chicago a crimestopping program called "Operation Block-watch." One of the leaders is Marion Munnich, a housewife and SON/SOC member who lives on the southwest side with her husband Rich and two small children. She explains: "People begin a blockwatch program by first meeting at a neighbor's home. There they are given organizing materials [written in English, Spanish and Polish] and phone numbers of law enforcement and government agencies." Munnich says, "It's a way average people can get their block back even if they have to deal with gangs."

Education: SON/SOC helped initiate Chicagoans United to Reform Education (CURE) — a multiracial organization headed by former State Supt. of Education Michael J. Bakalis, now dean of education at Loyola University of Chicago. CURE proposes the establishment of local school governing councils with elected community, parent and teacher representatives. These councils would have the power to hire principals and teachers and to set the curriculum and budget.

Thus the clash. Is it race? Yes. Is it economic gerrymandering? Absolutely yes! Is it fair? No! — to both sides.

Opponents of SON/SOC and GHEP are not without strong views of their own. According to Northeastern University Professor Robert Starks, a well-known black activist and chairman of the Committee on Black Political Empowerment, "Both sides need a common dialogue to get beyond racism and code words." He respects SON/SOC's fights against redlining and banking abuses but warns that these people "are victims of their own mythmaking" and that they should "join with potential black movers into their neighborhoods to fight racism and discrimination." Other foes, like 15th Ward Ald. Marlene Carter, a black whose ward includes some SON/SOC neighborhoods, reject the concept of GHEP. Carter says, "There is no need to stabilize housing values because they are not declining."

To be sure, many blacks are moving slowly up the economic ladder in Chicago. But there are fewer neighborhoods today than in the past where middle-income working people can afford to live. Moreover, because of past racial differences, there is no record or evidence in Chicago that integrated working-class neighborhoods can survive. Thus SON/SOC is on the firing line.

Allies of SON/SOC see a difficult road ahead. According to Bill Higginson, former vice president of Chicago United and a key player in efforts to resolve SON/SOC's differences with Washington back in 1983: "It will be difficult for SON/SOC to gain wide acceptance, even though they have a diverse and positive agenda on critical citywide issues. The racist tag is difficult to lose even if it doesn't fit." Conservatives like Roeser see a liberal bias against SON/SOC and white ethnics. He says: "If a community of blacks were trying to preserve their neighborhoods, these liberal community groups and the liberal media would be saluting them." And according to an influential insider on the Chicago fundraising scene, who wished to remain anonymous: "Many foundations will not support a community organization like SON/SOC because it has an all-white board. They would not apply this principle to a group with an all-black board. White ethnic has become a pejorative term in Chicago."

In Alinksy's words: "Power is not only what you have but what the enemy thinks you have." SON/SOC members have come to believe, especially after the death of Mayor Washington last November, that the chances for GHEP passage in Chicago's fluid political situation are limited. The coalition's one remaining trump card was to tell white-ethnic Democratic elected officials that either they go all-out for home equity or else the SON/SOC communities will go over to the Republican party.

In the past, Democratic officials, most of whom were never SON/SOC supporters, would have scoffed at such an ultimatum from a group outside of the regular party organization. But these are new times. The phrase "Chicago Republican" is no longer an oxymoron. Moreover, because of the city's changing demographics, ethnic Democratic pols now realize that they cannot afford to lose any sizable chunk from their vote base. They take SON/SOC's threat seriously, especially when they see the coalition's new GHEP button. It reads: "Home Equity Or Else" — and shows a picture of an upside down donkey.

On February 1, House Speaker Michael J. Madigan (also Democratic committeeman of the southwest side's 13th Ward) held an extraordinary meeting of state and city elected officials at the State of Illinois Center in Chicago. A few days earlier Madigan had announced his support for GHEP and had promised that if the City Council refused to deal with this issue, he would introduce state legislation preempting the city on home equity.

At the speaker's meeting Mayer laid down SON/SOC's terms: "For years, our people believed they have had a contract with the Democratic party. However, if there is no support on this home equity issue, then we believe that the contract has been broken." In the ensuing discussions, white and black speakers divided along racial lines. Neither side was able to see that they were far closer to being allies than adversaries.

In many ways the organizing efforts of the Southwest Parish and Neighborhood Federation and the Northwest Neighborhood Federation have been a huge success. By uniting under the SON/SOC banner, they now reflect the views and concerns of a vast percentage of Chicago's white ethnics. Yet their original goal of gaining power and respect for their communities remains as elusive as ever. The only real change is that under Daley they felt ignored, while under Washington and his successor, Acting Mayor Eugene Sawyer, they fear for their neighborhoods' very survival. White ethnics in Chicago have become a convenient scapegoat for various groups — white and black. Yuppies and lakefronters can maintain their economically segregated neighborhoods by pushing the issue of racial discrimination on the backs of the southwest and northwest side ethnics, while black leaders can score political points by dismissing the legitimate concerns of white ethnics as racist rhetoric.

The historic resegregation trails on the southside's major east-west thoroughfares (55th, 63rd, 71st, etc.) are now considered insufficient evidence to support neighborhood stabilization efforts — even though meaningful integration of Chicago's working-class white and black families is taking place only in SON/SOC communities. Erik Wogstad, SON/SOC's home equity project director, sums up ethnic frustrations: "Race intimidates the political power structure and frightens off white liberal organizational support. . . . [To them] we are funny neighborhoods that no one has to respond to." We shall see.

Why Organize?
Problems and Promise in the
Inner City

by Barack Obama

'Nowhere is the promise of organizing more
apparent than in the traditional black churches.'
Barack Obama

Photo courtesy of Developing Communities Project

O ver the past five years, I've often had a difficult time explaining my profession to folks. Typical is a remark a public school administrative aide made to me one bleak January morning, while I waited to deliver some flyers to a group of confused and angry parents who had discovered the presence of asbestos in their school.

"Listen, Obama," she began. "You're a bright young man, Obama. You went to college, didn't you?"

I nodded.

"I just cannot understand why a bright young man like you would go to college, get that degree and become a community organizer."

"Why's that?"

" 'Cause the pay is low, the hours is long, and don't nobody appreciate you." She shook her head in puzzlement as she wandered back to attend to her duties.

I've thought back on that conversation more than once during the time I've organized with the Developing Communities Project, based in Chicago's far south side. Unfortunately, the answers that come to mind haven't been as simple as her question. Probably the shortest one is this: It needs to be done, and not enough folks are doing it.

The debate as to how black and other dispossessed people can forward their lot in America is not new. From W.E.B. DuBois to Booker T. Washington to Marcus Garvey to Malcolm X to Martin Luther King, this internal debate has raged between integration and nationalism, between accommodation and militancy, between sit-down strikes and boardroom negotiations. The lines between these strategies have never been simply drawn, and the most successful black leadership has recognized the need to bridge these seemingly divergent approaches. During the early years

For three years Barack Obama was the director of Developing Communities Project, an institutionally based community organization on Chicago's far south side. He has also been a consultant and instructor for the Gamaliel Foundation, an organizing institute working throughout the Midwest. Currently he is studying law at Harvard University. "Why Organize? Problems and Promise in the Inner City" was first published in the August/September 1988 *Illinois Issues*.

of the Civil Rights movement, many of these issues became submerged in the face of the clear oppression of segregation. The debate was no longer whether to protest, but how militant must that protest be to win full citizenship for blacks.

Twenty years later, the tensions between strategies have reemerged, in part due to the recognition that for all the accomplishments of the 1960s, the majority of blacks continue to suffer from second-class citizenship. Related to this are the failures — real, perceived and fabricated — of the Great Society programs initiated by Lyndon Johnson. Facing these realities, at least three major strands of earlier movements are apparent.

First, and most publicized, has been the surge of political empowerment around the country. Harold Washington and Jesse Jackson are but two striking examples of how the energy and passion of the Civil Rights movement have been channeled into bids for more traditional political power. Second, there has been a resurgence in attempts to foster economic development in the black community, whether through local entrepre-neurial efforts, increased hiring of black contractors and corporate managers, or Buy Black campaigns. Third, and perhaps least publicized, has been grass-roots community organizing, which builds on indigenous leadership and direct action.

Proponents of electoral politics and economic development strategies can point to substantial accomplishments in the past 10 years. An increase in the number of black public officials offers at least the hope that government will be more responsive to inner-city constituents. Economic development programs can provide structural improvements and jobs to blighted communities.

In my view, however, neither approach offers lasting hope of real change for the inner city unless undergirded by a systematic approach to community organization. This is because the issues of the inner city are more complex and deeply rooted than ever before. Blatant discrimination has been replaced by institutional racism; problems like teen pregnancy, gang involvement and drug abuse cannot be solved by money alone. At the same time, as Professor William Julius Wilson of the University of Chicago has pointed out, the inner city's economy and its government support have declined, and middle-class blacks are leaving the neighbor-hoods they once helped to sustain.

Neither electoral politics nor a strategy of economic self-help and internal development can by themselves respond to these new challenges. The election of Harold Washington in Chicago or of Richard Hatcher in Gary were not enough to bring jobs to inner-city neighborhoods or cut a 50 percent drop-out rate in the schools, although they did achieve an important symbolic effect. In fact, much-needed black achievement in prominent city positions has put us in the awkward position of administer-ing underfunded systems neither equipped nor eager to address the needs of the urban poor and being forced to compromise their interests to more powerful demands from other sectors.

Self-help strategies show similar limitations. Although both laudable and necessary, they too often ignore the fact that without a stable community, a well-educated population, an adequate infrastructure and an informed and employed market, neither new nor well-established companies will be willing to base themselves in the inner city and still compete in the international marketplace. Moreover, such approaches can and have become thinly veiled excuses for cutting back on social programs, which are anathema to a conservative agenda.

In theory, community organizing provides a way to merge various strategies for neighborhood empowerment. Organizing begins with the premise that (1) the problems facing inner-city communities do not result from a lack of effective solutions, but from a lack of power to implement these solutions; (2) that the only way for communities to build long-term power is by organizing people and money around a common vision; and (3) that a viable organization can only be achieved if a broadly based indigenous leadership — and not one or two charismatic leaders — can knit together the diverse interests of their local institutions.

This means bringing together churches, block clubs, parent groups and any other institutions in a given community to pay dues, hire organizers, conduct research, develop leadership, hold rallies and education campaigns, and begin drawing up plans on a whole range of issues — jobs, education, crime, etc. Once such a vehicle is formed, it holds the power to make politicians, agencies and corporations more responsive to community needs. Equally important, it enables people to break their crippling isolation from each other, to reshape their mutual values and expectations and rediscover the possibilities of acting collaboratively — the prerequisites of any successful self-help initiative.

By using this approach, the Developing Communities Project and other organizations in Chicago's inner city have achieved some impressive results. Schools have been made more accountable; job training programs have been established; housing has been renovated and built; city services have been provided; parks have been refurbished; and crime and drug problems have been curtailed. Additionally, plain folk have been able to access the levers of power, and a sophisticated pool of local civic leadership has been developed.

But organizing the black community faces enormous problems as well. One problem is the not entirely undeserved skepticism organizers face in many communities. To a large degree, Chicago was the birthplace of community organizing, and the urban landscape is littered with the skeletons of previous efforts. Many of the best-intentioned members of the community have bitter memories of such failures and are reluctant to muster up renewed faith in the process.

A related problem involves the aforementioned exodus from the inner city of financial resources, institutions, role models and jobs. Even in areas that have not been completely devastated, most households now stay afloat with two incomes. Traditionally, community organizing has drawn support from women, who due to tradition and social discrimination had the time and the inclination to participate in what remains an essentially voluntary activity. Today the majority of women in the black community work full time, many are the sole parent, and all have to split themselves between work, raising children, running a household and maintaining some semblance of a personal life — all of which makes voluntary activities lower on the priority list. Additionally, the slow exodus of the black middle class into the suburbs means that people shop in one neighborhood, work in another, send their child to a school across town and go to church someplace other than the place where they live. Such geographical dispersion creates real problems in building a sense of investment and common purpose in any particular neighborhood.

Finally community organizations and organizers are hampered by their own dogmas about the style and substance of organizing. Most still practice what Professor John McKnight of Northwestern University calls a "consumer advocacy" approach, with a focus on wrestling services and resources from the ouside powers that be. Few are thinking of harnessing the internal productive capacities, both in terms of money and people, that already exist in communities.

Our thinking about media and public relations is equally stunted when compared to the high-powered direct mail and video approaches successfully used by conservative organizations like the Moral Majority. Most importantly, low salaries, the lack of quality training and ill-defined possibilities for advancement discourage the most talented young blacks from viewing organizing as a legitimate career option. As long as our best and brightest youth see more opportunity in climbing the corporate ladder than in building the communities from which they came, organizing will remain decidedly handicapped.

None of these problems is insurmountable. In Chicago, the Developing Communities Project and other community organizations have pooled resources to form cooperative think tanks like the Gamaliel Foundation. These provide both a formal setting where experienced organizers can rework old models to fit new realities and a healthy environment for the recruitment and training of new organizers. At the same time the leadership vacuum and disillusionment following the death of Harold Washington have made both the media and people in the neighborhoods more responsive to the new approaches community organizing can provide.

Nowhere is the promise of organizing more apparent than in the traditional black churches. Possessing tremendous financial resources, membership and — most importantly — values and biblical traditions that call for empowerment and liberation, the black church is clearly a slumbering giant in the political and economic landscape of cities like

Chicago. A fierce independence among black pastors and a preference for more traditional approaches to social involvement (supporting candidates for office, providing shelters for the homeless) have prevented the black church from bringing its full weight to bear on the political, social and economic arenas of the city.

Over the past few years, however, more and more young and forward-thinking pastors have begun to look at community organizations such as the Developing Communities Project in the far south side and GREAT in the Grand Boulevard area as a powerful tool for living the social gospel, one which can educate and empower entire congregations and not just serve as a platform for a few prophetic leaders. Should a mere 50 prominent black churches, out of the thousands that exist in cities like Chicago, decide to collaborate with a trained organizing staff, enormous positive changes could be wrought in the education, housing, employment and spirit of inner-city black communities, changes that would send powerful ripples throughout the city.

In the meantime, organizers will continue to build on local successes, learn from their numerous failures and recruit and train their small but growing core of leadership — mothers on welfare, postal workers, CTA drivers and school teachers, all of whom have a vision and memories of what communities can be. In fact, the answer to the original question — why organize? — resides in these people. In helping a group of housewives sit across the negotiating table with the mayor of America's third largest city and hold their own, or a retired steelworker stand before a TV camera and give voice to the dreams he has for his grandchild's future, one discovers the most significant and satisfying contribution organizing can make.

In return, organizing teaches as nothing else does the beauty and strength of everyday people. Through the songs of the church and the talk on the stoops, through the hundreds of individual stories of coming up from the South and finding any job that would pay, of raising families on threadbare budgets, of losing some children to drugs and watching others earn degrees and land jobs their parents could never aspire to — it is through these stories and songs of dashed hopes and powers of endurance, of ugliness and strife, subtlety and laughter, that organizers can shape a sense of community not only for others, but for themselves.

Tenants and Neighbors battle HUD and ComEd

by Thom Clark

'If evictions or rent increases were going to happen to them, then it could happen to us.'
Linda Roberts

While shopping at a corner grocery store in Chicago's West Town community last spring, Luis Rodriguez eyed "an alarming flier" on the front counter. It said, "There's a killer in your alley." The flier was issued by the 25-year-old Northwest Community Organization (NCO). It explained that a site on his block was contaminated with PCBs, a highly toxic lubricant once used by electric utilities but now banned. The flier called residents to a community meeting to learn more.

Raised in the infamous Hell's Kitchen neighborhood of New York City, Rodriguez was no stranger to urban problems but had never gotten involved before. Finding it difficult to get a job in New York after gaining an education degree, he moved to Chicago last year, into the West Town building owned by his family for over 17 years. "With time on my hands while looking for work," Rodriguez recalls, he decided to go to the NCO meeting with some neighbors.

Nick Iakovos was also introduced to community organizing via a piece of paper. One morning last January, Nick and his wife Carmen found a 30-day notice from their landlord slipped under the door of their two-bedroom apartment in a high-rise in Chicago's Uptown neighborhood. The notice sought a 40 percent rent increase from the 14-year residents of 833 West Buena. The landlord was demanding that the five-member Iakovos family take a larger three-bedroom apartment, or move. The owners of the federally financed building had recently prepaid their 40-year FHA mortgage, believing this action released them from federal rent regulations in the speculation-ridden Uptown housing market.

"There was something fishy here," Nick recalls. His family had been good tenants: "I never got in trouble here." So Nick brought his notice to a

Thom Clark teaches at the Community Media Workshop at Malcolm X College where he trains community groups in the ways of the media. A freelance editor and photographer with 16 years experience in Chicago's neighborhood development movement, Clark was editor of *The Neighborhood Works* and has also been director of the Chicago Rehab Network and Voice of the People in Uptown. "Tenants and Neighbors Battle HUD and ComEd" was first published in the December 1988 *Illinois Issues*.

local group he had heard his sister-in-law talk about, Organization of the North-East (ONE), a 15-year-old community organization serving the Uptown and Edgewater areas on Chicago's north lakefront.

What Rodriguez and Iakovos learned and the processes they found themselves caught up in changed their views on the ability of a community to move large institutions. The stories that follow tell about campaigns by two community organizations on two different issues. Iakovos became involved in ONE's effort to avail low-income renters of the protections afforded by the federal Emergency Housing Act. Rodriguez became part of NCO's drive to force Commonwealth Edison to inform local communities about its toxic spills. Both stories show how ordinary citizens brought accountability to the powers that be.

When Iakovos visited ONE's office, news of his eviction notice from a federally financed building was no surprise. Felecia Mitchell-Bute, an organizer with ONE and also with the Uptown Tenants Union, had been alerted to the problem in the spring of 1987. The city faced the potential loss of over 10,000 units of affordable housing through prepayment of FHA mortgages. Over 2,000 units of affordable housing in Uptown faced this demise by 1994. The disclosure was reported in *The Network Builder*, the newsletter of the Chicago Rehab Network, a citywide housing development coalition.

The FHA mortgages derived from a federal program. The government had offered private investors 40-year loans at 1 to 3 percent interest. In return, investors had to agree to rent the housing to low- and moderate-income tenants for 20 years. Owners would then have the option of continuing the arrangement or of prepaying the remaining mortgage. Prepayment would free owners to do what they wished with the property.

In Uptown, Mitchell-Bute had a ONE college intern survey the owners of HUD buildings. The survey found that most were going to prepay, believing that this would enable them to charge market rents or sell their buildings for a higher price.

To ascertain the best response to the pending wholesale evictions, ONE organizers met with an ad hoc citywide coalition of FHA building tenants, with other area groups who made up the Uptown Task Force on Displacement and Housing, and with attorney Dan Burke of the Legal Assistance Foundation. Burke informed them of pending federal legislation that would preclude or severely limit the prepayment option for owners, and he encouraged them to start working with tenants of the affected buildings.

Mitchell-Bute and Susan Gahm, another ONE organizer and member of the Uptown Tenants Union, began contacting tenants in HUD buildings, but not at the Buena building because the ONE organizers thought another organization was working with its tenants.

At a HUD building at Sheridan and Gunnison that faced prepayment in January 1989, ONE organizers contacted Linda Roberts. She had lived in

Gunnison for 13 years and was part of a previous FHA tenants union that had fought rent increases in her building. "We would go over the owners' profit and loss statements with a fine-tooth comb. The figures didn't add up. Our rent money wasn't going to claimed higher taxes and fuel bills, much less into our building," Roberts says.

When ONE's Uptown Tenants Union (UTU) came to Roberts' building, the FHA tenants union saw it as an opportunity. "We wanted to hook up because our previous union couldn't survive off of member fees collected. We learned about the prepayment option pending on our building and decided to again try and find the owner and sit down to negotiate options, including giving us six months' notice. I had the fact sheets and files on the building, but without UTU, I'd be at wit's end. I didn't know how the FHA worked. I would have been fighting a meaningless game." Uptown Tenants Union in fact, had made contact with tenants like Roberts in several HUD buildings. Numbering some 350 members, Uptown Tenants Union began filling up file drawers with tenant assistance intake forms. "We targeted four buildings in particular with upcoming prepayment option dates," recalls Gahm.

By the time Nick Iakovos arrived at ONE's office with his notice from the Buena building landlord, the organization knew what to do. ONE organizers immediately paid a visit to the regional office of the U.S. Department of Housing and Urban Development (HUD). Interviews with key HUD staff and searches through HUD records revealed important information. Prepayment on Buena had been quietly accepted by the agency on January 4, 1988, only one day before the owners' legal 20-year anniversary date and just weeks after congressional approval of the legislation Burke had been talking about — the Emergency Low-Income Housing Preservation Act of 1987.

Among other provisions, the act effectively precluded any prepayment of the FHA mortgages for two years. It required HUD to negotiate with building owners, provide vouchers to maintain affordable units, and otherwise certify that prepayment would not disrupt local housing. HUD had performed none of these tasks before accepting the Buena prepayment.

"HUD clearly goofed on this one," Burke asserted at the time, and within days one of the congressional sponsors of the act agreed. In February, invited to speak at a citywide conference of Chicago's FHA tenants, U.S. Rep. Barney Frank (D.-Mass.) said: "This is clearly a situation the new law was supposed to prevent. [HUD's action] represents a continuation of a national trend causing an upsurge in homelessness."

"We had to get into the building to inform tenants of their rights, before people started to move out," Mitchell-Bute recalls. Working with Nick and Carmen Iakovos and over 60 other tenants from the 209-unit Buena building, ONE leafleted apartments. It also brought legal aide attorneys to several evening meetings at a local church hall to interview tenants and began planning a demonstration against HUD to force agency compliance with the new law. "When we learned about Buena," recalls Roberts, "we just had to plug in. We didn't want another HUD building in the neighborhood to slip through the cracks. If [evictions or rent increases] were going to happen to them, then it could happen to us."

Dozens of sign-carrying Uptown tenants picketed the HUD regional office February 22, 1988. When representatives of ONE's Uptown Tenants Union met with HUD regional director Gertrude Jordan, they learned that local HUD officials were "not in a position to do anything." Media coverage was intensive. The next day, Burke filed suit in federal court on behalf of the Buena tenants, seeking a stay of the eviction notices and return of the mortgage prepayment to the owners. This was the first test case nationally under the new law. The court granted a temporary reprieve to the tenants. The final outcome of the suit is still pending.

HUD officials were not suprised with the court action. According to HUD's Jim Zale, "We knew the Emergency Housing Act would generate a lot of lawsuits because it reneges on some long-held owner rights for prepayment." But as acting housing director of HUD's regional office at the time of the tenants' demonstration, Zale also felt that the meeting in Jordan's office was "very productive." He says, "We were dealing with forces that none of us could control. The tenants were very professional and knowledgable. As is often the case, they had looked into this legislation better than we had."

How does Nick Iakovos feel now? "I believe the law will protect me," he says. "You have to be willing to get in there and play the game. We're no lawyers, but [the owners] tried to evict us and then they backed off." Carmen Iakovos believes the HUD demonstration was critical to convincing people "that the only way to resolve our problem is to stay together."

Buena tenants continued to meet over the summer and participated in another affordable housing demonstration in July at the nearby home of Gov. James R. Thompson. "We're holding stable," Carmen says, "everything's quiet in the building." Nick believes the building's owners are just waiting until after the November election before they make their next move. He says, "I got in here 14 years ago when things weren't so good in the neighborhood. Now it's improving and they want us out. I won't give up on myself."

Like ONE, the Northwest Community Organization (NCO) is a veteran of many organizing battles. In its West Town/Humboldt Park neighborhood, it is best known for its education, housing and development organizing, but its entree into environmental concerns did not begin with the PCB problem on Luis Rodriguez's block. A few years before, a fire in an abandoned factory had spewed toxic-laden waste water into the alley and backyard of longtime NCO leader Dorothy Meada. NCO took up the fight to force a cleanup involving both the U.S. and Illinois Environmental Protection agencies. It also led a campaign through the Chicago City

Council to enact more stringent environmental legislation.

"If it hadn't been for Dorothy's fire," recalls Faith Urrutia, another NCO leader, "I wouldn't have paid much attention to the men in moon-suits going down my alley last March." The team of moon-suits left an excavated site, marked by street sawhorses, yellow and black warning tape, and "a little sign I took the trouble to read," Urrutia says. In obtuse legalese, the sign declared the excavation to be a PCB site and directed further inquiries to Commonwealth Edison or the Coast Guard. Urrutia called ComEd and stopped by the NCO office to report her discovery.

NCO staff director Kim McReynolds assigned a college intern to the case. After filing a Freedom of Information request with the U.S. Environmental Protection Agency (USEPA), Urrutia and the intern were soon thumbing through agency files downtown. They found that ComEd had submitted to a 1986 consent decree to clean up 492 PCB-contaminated sites in the Chicago metro area. The contamination was caused by utility pole capacitor explosions, some dating as far back as 1978. By the spring of 1988, only one-third of the sites had been cleaned, most of them in suburban areas.

"We knew we had stumbled onto something," McReynolds says. Though the USEPA files were disorganized, NCO determined that West Town/Humboldt Park contained 14 sites scattered over five wards. McReynolds brought the issue to NCO's executive board to consider the best approach. "With [ComEd's] pending rate increase request and expiring franchise with Chicago, the way NCO cut the issue and how ComEd handled it could mean a lot," she explains.

With board approval, McReynolds sought technical expertise from two nonprofit corporations: Citizens for a Better Environment and the Center for Neighborhood Technology. She also sought legal assistance from Howard Learner of Business and Professional People in the Public Interest, known for its years of litigation against ComEd on nuclear plants and rate issues. Learner agreed to assist NCO, not in a lawsuit but in an organizing campaign.

Luis Rodriguez and his neighbors came to one of NCO's informational meetings. He learned he was living 150 feet from a capacitor that had blown up eight years before. Though the site had been initially "cleaned" four years ago, the federal standard for an acceptable PCB level had been lowered in the interim. Rodriguez was concerned. (Indeed, subsequent testing of the site near his home as the NCO campaign got underway revealed further PCB contamination.)

But it was not health concerns that galvanized the community. McReynolds says, "What finally clicked in the minds of community people was the right to know. ComEd acted as if the community couldn't handle the information, and this made people angry. Furthermore, cleanup costs had been built into ComEd's rate base, and people didn't think utility customers should have to pay for ComEd's mistakes."

NCO's community meetings led to a public hearing with ComEd representatives August 1. A careful press strategy was mapped out beforehand with Business and Professional People in the Public Interest. As a result, the story of ComEd's slow cleanup was in the media before the meeting was held. The media coverage "shook up ComEd," McReynolds recalls. Utility representatives were "responding to our issue, not the other way around. They found an informed panel of community residents unwilling to accept the utility's P.R. assurances that all was okay."

The meeting attracted not only NCO old-line leaders and newly involved residents like Rodriguez, but also union activists, environmental groups and other community groups from around the city. "We were not only demanding that ComEd clean up the PCB sites we'd discovered in West Town, but also that they release a citywide list of sites. We didn't want ComEd to set neighborhood [against] neighborhood," McReynolds says. A slide show of the sites, testimony from a toxicologist and attorney Learner, and informed questions from a vocal crowd made for "a fact-filled, exciting meeting," McReynolds recalls. "ComEd responded with some stupid statements from a P.R. point of view." The next day, ComEd released a list of all the sites to the *Chicago Tribune*.

"ComEd started backing down because we had a plan," Rodriguez says. "I would have thought that with their franchise expiring with the city, they'd be doing all they could to get public opinion on their side, that they'd be doing the site cleanups better than the law required. But they sure were taking their time."

ComEd spokesman Mike Kelly disagrees. "When we first became aware of the NCO campaign in the newspapers, most of the cleanup of the PCB sites in that area was completed." Cleanup had begun during 1987 in two of ComEd's six operating divisions, one in the western suburbs, the other on the city's north side, "not in response to any perceived demand by one community group over another," according to Kelly, but for logistical reasons. Kelly says that under the USEPA consent decree ComEd has until 1991 to complete the cleanup program.

Within days of the original spills starting in the 1970s, all of the sites had been cleaned, Kelly explains. And while ComEd agreed under the consent decree to reclean the sites when the federal standard changed, Kelly says, "we didn't feel the hazard posed any danger to the areas surrounding the spills. Instead of arguing over how clean is clean, we agreed to go back and resurvey the sites and reclean to the new standard. It's a model program. We're the only utility in the nation cleaning up to this standard."

Once NCO had the site locations, it turned to City Hall on the remaining issues: the cleanup schedules and proper site signs. Initial meetings between community leaders and city bureaucrats were tense. The city wanted to research the question further; NCO produced the research it had already completed. NCO sent letters to every alderman whose ward contained PCB sites, as well as to community groups in the affected areas. By fall 1988, organizations around the city were clamoring for City Hall to take action.

Follow-up testing of the sites began (with two of nine previously "cleaned" sites found to have PCB levels over the EPA-mandated minimum). As of the end of October, according to Kelly, ComEd had some 20 sites left on the south side and was doing all it could to accelerate the cleanup of all the sites in the city during the coming year.

Agreement on signs came after a series of meetings held with the city and community groups, including NCO. ComEd agreed to "install signs at spill sites which still had to be cleaned, which had not been identified prior to that," says ComEd's Kelly. While waiting for a decision, some members of the NCO planning committee designed their own PCB-site warning sign and had it printed and distributed.

For ComEd, Kelly says, this PCB cleanup was more than an environmental issue. "It even becomes a political issue in a city that's as politicized as Chicago," Kelly says. "ComEd is an easy target, but we don't feel there's anything to be ashamed of with the way we've conducted this cleanup."

For Luis Rodriguez, NCO's campaign against ComEd was exhilarating. Now a special education teacher in a local school, Rodriguez has backed off some on his involvement as the West Town sites were cleaned and other groups around the city picked up on the issue. "The exposure gave me a thrill," he says of the media coverage, including several radio interviews. "What gave me a real kick was when ComEd started to back down."

For Urrutia, the battle with ComEd isn't over. Other city sites need cleaning and retesting. "My role now is to back up other groups, to let them know we got it done, so they can too," she says. "ComEd's arrogance as a monopoly must be considered in light of ongoing franchise negotiations," she says. Both NCO and ONE launched successful petition drives in their wards over the summer to put an advisory referendum on the ComEd franchise on the November ballot. The referenda were approved overwhelmingly. Though not binding, the message was clear: The city should bargain tough with ComEd.

For McReynolds the PCB campaign opened up new possibilities. "Organizer friends of mine didn't think NCO had any business in environmental issues," she says. But unlike traditional NCO campaigns around affordable housing or appropiate redevelopment planning, "the press we got allowed us to cut across block boundaries and class lines in a way that's difficult with other issues." Solid research plus planning the strategy with both old and new community leaders, McReynolds believes, "made it easier for people to accept an organization being agressive with a major institution."

Effective use of the media was key to NCO's success. Community organizations are usually trying, according to McReynolds, "to make good with the bad press we get, but here we had good coverage, even from the *Tribune*." Later the *Tribune* attacked NCO in its "New Politics of Poverty" series as being part of a citywide anti-development cabal. McReynolds believes that characterization is unfair. Though ONE was also pilloried in the series, its Buena campaign against HUD benefited from good print and broadcast coverage.

Community organizing, according to its proponents, "is a process by which exploited people learn to employ the tools of a democratic society" ("Alinsky's legacy," *Illinois Issues*, January 1988). Simply put, the success of these two campaigns hinged on careful and expert execution of what many activists once called "Alinsky-style" organizing: Identify the problem, research the issue to find the opportunity, find and educate leaders and plan an action against a targeted personality or institution.

Each organization has relied on support and leadership from a local church base, as did Saul Alinsky's own early efforts in Chicago and Rochester, N.Y. But both have moved beyond these institutional constituencies to other networks and interest groups, such as tenants. Each secured assistance from outside experts — attorneys, environmental activists, citywide and national coalitions. Each organization found new leaders and members through the campaigns. Last May both Uptown Tenants Union member Roberts and NCO leader Urrutia attended the National Peoples Action conference in Washington, D.C., where they strategized with other community leaders on HUD and EPA problems.

For NCO, the success against ComEd strengthens its hand. "We made valuable new contacts in the community," McReynolds reports. NCO's "31-flavor mix" of organizing on housing, education, crime, utility and job issues

---

Funds and staff for organizing

Both Northwest Community Organization (NCO) and Organization of the NorthEast (ONE) operate on annual budgets of about $300,000, based on grants from foundations, corporations and the United Way. Both operate local outposts of the Chicago Energy Savers Fund, a successful low-interest loan program sponsored by the city and Peoples Gas. NCO's energy conservation effort generates one-third of its budget in fee-for-service income. Including other loan programs administered through its NorthEast Investment Center, ONE's fee income covers half its operating budget.

Both organizations carry four full-time organizers and make effective use of college intern programs. Both struggle for general operating support to cover unexpected issues. "Without our ongoing contributions from local businesses, we would be hard-pressed to take on sudden campaigns like the PCB/ComEd project," NCO's Kim McReynolds explains.

"sometimes makes a very messy sundae," according to McReynolds. But the campaign cut across all these issues, and positive press coverage brought NCO's success to the attention of far more people than it generally gets.

For ONE, the Buena building campaign gave a tremendous boost to its Uptown Tenants Union and its work in other HUD high-rises facing similar pressures for conversion to market-rate rentals. New alliances were cemented with sometimes competing groups, and the public became more aware of the possible loss of affordable housing. According to Gahm, the tenants that ONE is working with now realize they can avoid disruption to their families. "They're realizing they have nowhere else to go, so they better organize and fight potential eviction," she says.

For Mitchell-Bute the campaign revealed what tenants can do. Now working on development programs in Cabrini-Green public housing on Chicago's near north side, she recalls that the Buena situation almost got away from the organizers. Delays occurred while turf battles between area community groups were sorted out. "We realized [ONE] didn't have the staff to canvass a 200-plus unit building with less than a month to go before evictions. We had to turn it over to the tenants. This ultimately was the most important thing we did because as the tenants took over the canvass work, they developed relationships with each other, which is why there is still a core left of tenant leaders to persevere with the court fight."

The future of community organizing requires a return to some basics developed by Alinsky, Mitchell-Bute believes: "We've gotten so far from where Saul started — grass-roots leadership. We've had this dialogue in the last five years in Chicago about leadership development and nonprofits. But the reality is the leaders are now beginning to look like staff. Our leadership development arguments got us to the point where we got too lazy to do what needed to be done, and we started relying on staff to be leaders, or we brought in staff from other groups to represent their constituencies." Buena was a good example of this, she says. "When we walked into our first organizing meeting, all of us in the room were paid staff from one group or another."

The same thing happened in City Hall after Harold Washington was elected, she says. "We just looked at everybody brought in as paid staff. We didn't build on that empowerment movement. After he died and paid staff started leaving the Hall, everybody was looking for the grass-roots movement again."

What does she think now? "I feel good about Buena," Mitchell-Bute concludes. "The people there made the difference. We bought them time and if, as paid staff, we aren't there the next time, at least those tenants will take their organizing experience with them into the next building."

Though trained to deal with people, a community organizer is more often guided by the flow of paper across her desk: newspaper clips and legal briefs, legislative summaries and grant proposals, computer printouts and quick-print leaflets. But as Mitchell-Bute will tell you, organizing these stacks of paper into nuggets of knowledge will not produce a successful campaign. Training effective grass-roots leaders like Luis Rodriguez and Nick Iakovos is the essential task.

Gale Cincotta and Heather Booth

by Patrick Barry

'My intent has always been to win. That's all.'
Gale Cincotta

*'And, of course, the main goal
is the transformation of society.'*
Heather Booth

Photos by ! ul L. Merideh

H eather Booth and Gale Cincotta. If you had just one word to describe them, "artists" would fit best. To most people their names mean no more than the titles of their organizations, Citizen Action and the National Training and Information Center. Yet they are two of the best organizers in the country, and you can find them, sometimes, in their Chicago headquarters: Booth working two phones at once under a timber-beamed ceiling, Cincotta at her corner desk looking over a roomful of organizers. In very different ways, each has harnessed "people power" and produced extraordinary results.

Booth is a tall, erect woman with a voice that she changes from supportive to demanding in the course of a sentence. She has built an organization of 1.75 million members that spans 24 states and routinely affects legislation and elects progressives to office. Cincotta is a heavy-jowled former housewife who is well-known in bank boardrooms around the country. Through a shrewd combination of confrontation and strong-arm legislation, she has forced banks to lend $1.6 *billion* in neighborhoods that need reinvestment.

The two are at the front of the latest and most powerful wave of organizing in U.S. history. Based out of Chicago like so many earlier organizing trailblazers, they have evolved from grass-roots troublemakers to national leaders, using tools ranging from legislative research and phone banks to winning smiles and a knack for negotiation. They don't work alone. They link up with others, provide training, hustle resources to keep the work going. Many of their associates have been with them since the civil rights days, providing a ready network of leadership, and both have cultivated allies in Congress, business, local government and the media. They have small armies at their command.

It is 30 hours after election night when Heather Booth, who had been

Patrick Barry is a Chicago free-lance writer who has been covering organizing and community and economic development since the early 1980s. He also been organizing in the recycling field for the last five years. "Heather Booth and Gale Cincotta: from Grass-roots Troublemakers to National Leaders" was first published in the January 1989 *Illinois Issues.*

working flat-out for the campaign of Michael Dukakis, takes the podium before 160 activist women in the Congress Hotel. The talk so far has been strained by disappointment over the Bush victory, and now Booth, in an emotional voice, is opening her soul: "I came here today because I wanted to be with friends and women and committed activists. . . . to see our way through."

Booth will admit later to a fierce and surprising anger at Dukakis for losing the big race, but instead of voicing that sentiment here, she injects steel into her voice and lays out a directive that goes something like this: "Let's keep it going because this battle is too important to lose." She will deliver variations on the speech four times in the next three days, each time describing what she calls a "progressive opening" in American politics. "I know the opening exists," she says later. "Whether we are strong enough to widen it and take advantage of it, I don't know."

Gale Cincotta is working her own magic at Chicago's Bismarck Hotel. It is November 14, 1988, the first day of a National Training and Information Center (NTIC) conference on housing issues, and Cincotta has a formidable lineup of speakers doing her work for her. One after another, top executives from Aetna Insurance, Harris Bank, BP America and Allstate Insurance Co. tell 350 listeners that the federal government must restore its commitment to housing programs for poor and moderate-income Americans. Edward Williams from Harris Bank even suggests that corporate America should link arms with community groups and go to Washington to demand renewed investment.

This same Edward Williams was once nose-to-nose with Cincotta, who had demanded inner-city investment by his bank and had helped pass a federal law to *make* him listen. Harris coughed up $35 million, and now that the former adversaries work together, the bank has pledged $50 million more. "She's crafty," says Williams. "She used to think you had to take someone around the neck and shake him until he said uncle. Now she realizes you can get as much done and faster by talking the issues through."

Cincotta laughs heartily at that story and suggests that it is the banking industry that has matured. She is still quite willing to get rough, as she did last May when she led several hundred people on four "hits" in Washington, D.C., one of them at the home of Sam Pierce, U.S. secretary of housing and urban development. The hits are a trademark technique of Cincotta's other organization, National People's Action, a loose coalition of grass-roots groups that converges on D.C. or another power center once a year for a big meeting and a day's worth of hits.

Cincotta, now in her mid-50s, cut her organizing teeth in the West Madison Street restaurant of her immigrant Greek and Latvian parents, where as an only child she listened to late-night discussions of class struggle, labor organizing and Depression-era survival. She married an auto mechanic and mothered six boys on Chicago's racially changing west side, discovering her knack for organizing in the early 1960s when she joined the PTA and almost instinctively put together a campaign to bring new resources into the neighborhood. She learned by listening and by doing her homework, and by being herself. "You should talk to anyone the way you usually talk; you don't have time or energy to be someone else. And you can't bow and scrape, or be awed. You might be remembered more if you deal with them straight."

Cincotta recalls an early fight over school policy when she came up against a reluctant mid-level administrator and told him, "Look, you're a nice man, but as long as you stand in the way we are going to pound on you." He got out of the way, and Cincotta was soon talking to the school superintendent and to Mayor Richard J. Daley. In the process she realized that organizing at the local level simply wasn't enough. Banks and mortgage companies were "redlining" her neighborhood; the school board was sending its resources into wealthier areas, and federal laws worked against local progress. What drove her early on? "Anger," she says. "Just anger."

In the mid-1960s she joined and eventually became president of the Organization for a Better Austin (OBA), where she met up with two professional organizers: Tom Gaudette and Shel Trapp. Gaudette, a student of Saul Alinsky and founder of both OBA and the Northwest Community Organization (NCO), now does consulting work with community groups nationwide. Trapp, who served as director of OBA and NCO, still works with Cincotta today. She says: "Tom would tell me that I was doing it all wrong, that I had too many demands. But I figured we should get as much as we could, so I would go into a meeting with the list and keep my thumb on the one we were discussing. If we got number one, I would move my thumb down to number two and it became number one."

She ended up breaking a lot of rules. She was a woman in a field dominated by male leaders, and she rejected Alinsky's dictum that problems should be approached on a strictly neighborhood basis. She and Trapp linked up with the Northwest Community Organization and then created a new group in the territory between, forging the first multi-neighborhood coalition in a city that is now webbed with such groups. "Gale's political maturity and insight are awesome," says Trapp, now staff director and chief trainer for NTIC. He praises Cincotta's singular ability to bring opposing forces together, as she did at the conference with big business and community groups, but says such alliances begin on a quite different note. "I don't recall a single victory that started with us being nice. It always starts with confrontation; you know, using a two-by-four to get the mule's attention. And if someone is screwing people over, Gale will come down with both feet and crush them."

It is a fitting image because Cincotta is a heavy woman who fuels herself through a four-hour, wide-ranging interview by sneaking candy from a drawer in her desk. But while she clearly enjoys storming bureaucrats' offices, her real strength shows up later at the follow-up meetings when she methodically uses the legislative process to control America's lifeblood: money.

She helped write and pass the federal Community Reinvestment Act of 1976, which requires financial institutions that are being bought or sold to prove that they lend money in the communities they serve. The law alone might have gone unenforced, but Cincotta sent her troops into the microfilm rooms of Chicago's City Hall, and they found enough evidence of inadequate lending to bring First National Bank of Chicago, Harris Bank and Northern Trust to the negotiating table. They pledged $185 million to get Cincotta and seven other groups off their backs. With that victory and related hard-won regulations like the federal Home Mortgage Disclosure Act, NTIC began a national training effort that has produced scores of agreements worth about $1.6 billion. "We didn't even know that our bank was being sold until Gale called us," says Steve Banker, executive director of the Southern Counties Action Movement in Herrin, which negotiated a $5 million pact with Boatmen's Bank of St. Louis. "Cincotta is a role model for us. She has shown us that the important thing about organizing is the details, like knowing how to get past security on a hit."

Critics say Cincotta has accomplished all this with a hit-or-miss program that does not truly represent a national constituency. NTIC gets by with a staff of 14 and an annual budget of $475,000, and National People's Action (NPA) does its work almost entirely at the grass-roots level, with just $25,000 to coordinate the annual leadership meeting and the big conference. And while member groups notch regular victories on issues ranging from toxic waste to farm policy, the main focus remains tight on lending, mortgage insurance and housing issues. Cincotta is unapologetic. "I've never had a grand plan to build the ultimate organization; my intent has always been to win, that's all." She smiles a great endearing smile that no doubt plays a key role in turning adversaries into allies. She likes the work, and she likes to win.

So does Heather Booth, but she goes about it in a different way. While both leaders are careful not to disparage the other, they are clearly at odds over strategies. They share common views on many of what Booth calls the bread-and-butter issues of modern America — toxic pollution, housing affordability, energy costs, health care — yet they haven't worked together since 1981, when NPA and the Booth-created Citizen/Labor Energy Coalition staged a joint confrontation at the American Petroleum Institute convention in Chicago. Booth chose not to comment on Cincotta's approach, but her followers were less reluctant. "The NPA people believe that if you have a big enough demonstration, it will change the world; we don't consider that an adequate approach," says John Cameron, associate director of the Illinois Public Action Council, one of Citizen Action's most powerful affiliates. "Our sense is that direct action works only if there are

100 voters behind every person at the action. You have to prove that on election day."

To do that, Booth and Citizen Action use phone banks, a national door-to-door canvass network, constituency research, and even "opposition research" (a.k.a. digging up dirt). In the process they have infiltrated America's other power base: government. By knocking on 20,000 doors every weeknight and making a million phone calls a year, Citizen Action affiliates raise $20 million per year and rack up impressive victories. In 1986, they backed 334 candidates nationwide and 260 of them won. More impressive yet is the progression of Citizen Action staffers and board members into local and national office. In 1986, 23 Citizen Action leaders were elected in 10 states, and seven more were elected the following year. Illinois Congressman Lane Evans (D-17, Rock Island) was one of the first victories, defeating an incumbent Republican in supposedly conservative western Illinois, and both U.S. Rep. Charles Hayes (D-1, Chicago) and U.S. Rep. Cardiss Collins (D-7, Chicago) are Illinois Public Action Council board members. "Heather combines idealism and strong convictions with an understanding of the nuts and bolts of the political scene; that's something a lot of the progressive groups can't do," says U.S. Sen. Paul Simon, who taps Booth's expertise regularly. "You can ask her what is going on in Idaho and she'll be able to tell you, and to connect you with some people there."

Booth, 43, has accomplished such feats in anything but a hit-or-miss fashion. She is a tightly wound thinker who works methodically, quickly and on a dozen projects at once. Her desk has four neat racks jammed with files, and two telephones which she often uses simultaneously and with remarkable calm. She is most of all a master strategist. "What Heather does very, very well is formulate a new direction and rally people around it," says Brad Karkkainen, an organizer for Citizen Action in the early '80s and now chief of staff for Chicago 49th Ward Ald. David Orr. "She is the one who is most often at the cutting edge of whatever is the newest thing. She reacts to a changing situation and formulates the new argument."

Her latest argument is that the enormous changes in the American workplace and family are driving a "populist progressive movement" that could grow into the new majority. She points to the continuing gains by progressives in local and national office; the advance of bills on toxics, health care and South Africa sanctions; and to a 1988 poll of 3,200 Citizen Action members that showed sweeping support for universal health insurance, expanded child care and parental leave programs, and stronger housing and poverty programs.

She says, "For the last eight years people's most decent feelings were put on ice; a new selfishness was encouraged. But I think that is changing." Booth's delivery is carefully paced and articulate, with regular pauses as if she tests sentences in her head before giving them voice. "It's funny. What

I'm talking about are these shifts in history, and when you're making history, it's hard to see that you're making it. In 1960 when I was picketing Woolworths [where southern stores wouldn't seat blacks], it was hard to know that a full-blown civil rights movement would sweep the country. In 1965 it was hard to imagine that there would be a woman's movement by 1970. Now in 1988 I think we are just a few years away from a new progressive opening in the country."

It is a bold pronouncement for a woman who, as Sen. Simon points out, does most of her work behind the scenes. After building the 1,200-employee machine of Citizen Action, it is as if she is afraid the tool will not be put to its proper use. But like Cincotta, Booth didn't start out with grand plans. Born in Mississippi and raised in Brooklyn, she jumped into a heavy schedule of civil rights work in 1963 at the University of Chicago. That included speaking tours for the Student Nonviolent Coordinating Committee and local organizing for Chicago's Coordinating Council of Community Organizations, headed by Al Raby. But her early work was straightforward, single-purpose: the boycott of Woolworths; Chicago civil rights activities; anti-war rallies; a 1965 sit-in at the University of Chicago health clinic after a friend, raped at knifepoint, was denied a gynecological exam. "With struggle," she says, "there was change."

But as the civil rights and anti-war movements lost steam, Booth was increasingly restless. She had settled into a mainstream publishing job, and for practical reasons that included two young sons and an unemployed husband, "had vowed to stay out of trouble." But when a co-worker's salary was cut to finance the raise of another worker, Booth rose up angry and led a union organizing drive that culminated in her getting fired. She filed suit for back pay, and when she won in 1972, she used the money to start an organizing training center called Midwest Academy. That was her launching pad.

"What happened over time was more wonderful than we expected," she says, laughing with satisfaction and fiddling with the fabric of her white corduroy dress. "Our first retreat was a small gathering in the woods, but by 1988 we had 1,800 people, and it was so high-spirited and energy-filled and dynamic." In the interim, Booth worked with and nurtured an ever-expanding team of leaders. Nationally they include Ira Arlook of the Ohio Public Interest Campaign, now executive director of Citizen Action; and William Winpisinger of the Machinists Union and William Hutton of the National Council of Senior Citizens, who at the height of the energy crisis brought their powerful constituencies into the Citizen/Labor Energy Coalition. In Chicago are Steve Max, Booth's director of training at Midwest Academy, and Paul Booth, her husband and teammate, who co-chaired the Citizens Action Program in the 1970s and now directs organizing in Illinois for AFSCME, the American Federation of State, County and Municipal Employees.

Part of Booth's magic is her habit of almost constantly dishing out compliments and thanks to activists around her; on the phone and at conferences, she listens well and almost always encourages further efforts in a sincere and supportive voice. She considers organizing work as a road to personal transformation and can tick off the names of people around the country who have bloomed in the heat of battle. She also keeps a keen eye on the larger picture and moves on when the next challenge becomes apparent, leaving behind a trained group of organizers drilled in three rules: 1) win change for people with *measurable* results; 2) organize to give power to others and to transform them so they deepen their commitment, and 3) build ongoing, financially stable institutions that become respected in the community. She stays loose enough to jump back to an area that needs shoring up, or to push into a ripe frontier. She exercises regularly, and in between the 17-hour-a-day busy periods, she rests with husband Paul. "Paul is wonderful," she says, opening herself up as she so often does. "Not only do we love each other but our relationship is based on a common set of commitments and values. We met at a sit-in against the war in Vietnam, so we understand the kind of life we each lead." They also schedule time together, including a weeklong vacation after the election. When asked where they are going, she laughs and declines comment.

It is nonetheless a good question. Where are Heather Booth and Gale Cincotta going? And as these artists of social change lead their troupes into the 1990s, will there be a symbiosis between the group that puts people in office and the one that pounds on government until it listens? Robert Kuttner, in his book *The Life of the Party: Democratic Prospects for 1988 and Beyond*, writes that Citizen Action and the similarly ambitious ACORN (Association of Community Organizations for Reform Now) "are rapidly becoming part of the *de facto* Democratic machinery.... and they are just now attaining full political maturity." Cincotta's alliance with big business and her clout with government is reaching a similar stage; when the NTIC conference on housing broke up, the framework for a $20 billion National Housing Trust Fund had been established, and the big banks and oil companies were on the team. Cincotta warned the crowd that "this one might take us a year or so to win," a time frame that she later admitted was wildly optimistic.

"If we won enough and got Utopia, maybe I could quit," she says. "But right now I have to wear blinders because of all the other problems; I wish there were more people to work on the hospital problems and recycling and other issues." Says Booth: "One thing about this work is that if you don't think it's fun and reinforcing, you should not do it because you *will* get burned out." She is thinking right now in terms of the next four years, a reasonable time frame, she figures, to widen the progressive opening. But she gives herself away when she uses a scrap of paper to sketch a chart showing Midwest Academy's progression of training. "The goals are over here," she says, "and of course the main goal is the transformation of society." Now *that* might take some time.

Organizing in South Suburban Islands of Poverty

by Bill Kemp

'How do you begin to attract people when their most pressing problems are on a day-to-day surviving level?'
David Whitaker

Photo by Paul Beaty

I n front of a large poster board covered with photographs, fliers and newspaper clippings, Joseph L. Hawkins carefully details the progress made over the last year. Hawkins, his deep voice matching his large stature, knows that he has made a difference. He and his supporters believe that they have slowed the growth of the "criminal element" in their community.

Hawkins and the 25 members at the March 2 meeting of I-Watch live in Phoenix, a small suburb 10 miles south of Chicago. They encourage the police department to enforce the curfew, and the members patrol the streets and carry two-way radios that provide an instant line to the village police. In many ways, their monthly meetings are probably like those of countless neighborhood crime prevention organizations that dot the suburban landscape. Friendly greetings, cake and coffee are interspersed with plans for fundraising activities and a membership drive.

But this is the suburban exception, not the rule. All-black and one of the poorest suburbs in metropolitan Chicago, Phoenix is dealing not with the occasional garage break-in, but rather with a growing number of abandoned houses and with it an accompanying rise in crime. Vacant housing in a community provides an ideal infrastructure for local crime, and I-Watch has worked with the police, water and health departments to shut down a number of suspected drug houses. In September a well-publicized march in front of a number of these houses brought the organization some local fame and admiration. Area papers praised the group's efforts, and the neighboring city of Harvey is organizing a similar group. In February, the group received a $2,500 grant from Thornton Township to purchase additional radio equipment.

Saul Alinsky, the "father" of community organizing, would most likely be at home in Phoenix and I-Watch. It is a village of single unit homes,

Bill Kemp is a staff writer at *Illinois Times*, an independent weekly newspaper in Springfield. Formerly a Public Affairs Reporting intern at *Illinois Issues*, Kemp grew up in Thornton, located in the heart of the south suburbs. "Community Organizing in South Suburban Islands of Poverty" was first published in the May 1989 *Illinois Issues*.

strong churches and a deep sense of community. Those are the ingredients Alinsky relied upon to create his style of democratic, locally based organizing. Hawkins and many of the members of I-Watch have lived in Phoenix their entire lives and understand community problems and the context in which they must be addressed. They thus have a direct stake in the successes or failures of their organization. I-Watch is community organzing on the most basic of levels. This is not the "ivory tower" organizing, with seminars, wealthy foundations and journal articles. Hawkins, a manager at the Acme Steel plant in neighboring Riverdale, is a community leader Alinsky would be comfortable with. When asked what has been the most important accomplishment of I-Watch, Hawkins is quick to reply that members now believe they have at least partial control over the direction in which their community is moving.

What works in Phoenix though, will not work elsewhere. Alinsky's approach to organizing is becoming increasingly outdated in the underclass neighborhoods of not only the inner city, but the suburbs as well. In addition, the newly emerging need to cross political, economic and racial boundries and create a sense of common purpose for the south suburban region as a whole is forcing organizers away from Alinsky and into uncharted territory. Organizations like I-Watch will always have a place in communities where the environment is conducive to such an approach. But the south suburbs are demonstrating that new avenues in community organizing must be explored.

Called the most racially, economically and culturally diverse suburban area in the nation, the south suburbs has a combined population greater than 550,000. Yet in many ways it is a forgotten region of the Chicago metro area. With the enormous growth of Lake and DuPage counties over the last decade, the communities south of Chicago remain to a large degree outside the economic boom spotlight. Over the past 15 years the area has struggled with a shrinking industrial job and tax base. Major employers, like the Ford Motor Co. stamping plant in Chicago Heights, have scaled back the payroll by 3,000. Others, like the Wisconsin Steel works on the southeast side of Chicago, have shut down completely. During the recession earlier this decade, more than 25,000 steel, chemical and auto jobs were lost. But the area is rebounding, with the unemployment rate today hovering near 5 percent. Aggressive economic development strategies by area leaders are winning back an estimated 2,000 manufacturing jobs a year.

Unfortunately, the recovery has bypassed south suburban communities like Blue Island, Robbins, Harvey, Ford Heights and sections of Chicago Heights. Today it is not unusual for some neighborhoods in these communities to have unemployment rates in excess of 50 percent. They mirror the poorest neighborhoods in Chicago. "The suburbs are still thought of as the green spot or the escape from Chicago. People have not come to grips with the idea that there can be a suburban area with serious problems," said Tom Brindisi of the Chicago Area Project, a nonprofit organization that works with youth.

Since the migration of the middle class from the inner city and the older black suburbs, the community fabric of church, family and working-class values has slowly unraveled, replaced by single-parent families, welfare dependency and crime. Institutions of family, church, schools and a sense of community pride, tools available 50 years ago to Alinsky in the working-class slums of Chicago's south side, are no longer present. Although the Alinsky goal of fostering grass-roots power is still desirable, the means to reach the goal have disappeared.

According to University of Chicago sociologist William Julius Wilson, the rise of the underclass, the poorest of the poor, is in part rooted in the victories of the civil rights movement. As strides were made in opening housing and job markets, middle-class blacks fled the old neighborhoods, taking their businesses and middle-class values with them. Coupled with their flight was the transformation of the U.S. economy from an industrial to a service sector base. With this change went the high paying, low-skilled manufacturing jobs, forcing up the unemployment rate in the inner city and many suburbs. Today, some neighborhoods in the south suburbs confront the same problems as inner city neighborhoods in Chicago, New York and Detroit. This is the new challenge for organizers. If community organizing is to come from the community, where is the base of support to be found?

David Whitaker, the executive director of the Chicago Area Project (CAP), acknowledges that the Alinsky model is outdated when addressing the problems of the underclass. "An organizer's responsibilty is to look for existing entities, institutions and power structures that are already there as a part of the inherent fabric of the community. Places [CAP] is going today — Alinsky has essentially no model of operating within a community as devastated as Robbins or Ford Heights. The [Alinsky] model just doesn't relate today," he said. Whitaker stressed that the Alinsky approach remains useful in neighborhoods with existing structures. For example, United Neighborhoods Organization in Chicago has made excellent use of the Catholic church fabric within the Hispanic communities. But in communities like Ford Heights, the remaining churches are losing their grip on the people.

Whitaker's organization, with a network of sites throughout Chicago, is one of the most active community organizations in the south suburbs. CAP maintains three sites in Chicago Heights and one in Robbins. Although CAP was created to address juvenile delinquency, in practice the sites handle a wide variety of community problems. After-school enrichment activities, counseling and job training are but a few of the services the group provides. Programs of the Chicago Heights Community Committee also help single mothers. Andrea Byers, a single mother with two children, is a volunteer aide at the committee's storefront headquarters. For three years she has helped the children with homework, arts and crafts and games. She said working with the committee has kept her active in the community and has increased her self-esteem. In addition, CAP organizers are now in the final stages of setting up what they hope will be a model project for Ford Heights.

Because CAP is focused on youth, the organization has been at the forefront of addressing the emerging needs of the underclass, which is made up in large part of children and teenagers. Founded by University of Chicago sociologist Clifford R. Shaw, CAP was based on the then-revolutionary belief that juvenile delinquency was rooted not exclusively in the personality of the child but rather in the environment surrounding the child. Shaw's earliest work was based in the Polish Russell Square community on Chicago's south side. Using the local Boys' Club as a starting point, Shaw organized the first CAP community committee. Later he introduced an inexperienced but energetic organizer named Saul Alinsky to the Back of the Yards neighborhood in the late 1930s. Though disputes between the two led to a formal separation, Shaw's teachings played an important role in the development of Alinsky's approach to organizing.

CAP is currently undertaking the initial steps to create sites in the northern suburb of Waukegan and a site to aid the poor in DuPage County. But the heart of CAP outside the Chicago city limits lies in the south suburbs. As a University of Chicago graduate in the Alinsky-Shaw tradition of community organizing, Whitaker sees both the advantages and disadvantages of working in a suburban setting.

One distinct advantage that the Chicago Heights committee has over any CAP site in Chicago is the accessibilty to local government. "It is amazing the relationship you can foster with the schools and park district. In Chicago we're tired of fighting the Park District, while in the Heights there are open channels," he said. Whitaker said CAP requests for access in low-income, minority neighborhoods for Chicago Park District facilities fell on deaf ears until recently. Chicago Heights Community Committee Director Thornal Washington said that although he may not always agree with park policy in Chicago Heights, he is never ignored. Washington's group makes use of park district buildings and picnic areas.

Like CAP in Chicago Heights, I-Watch in Phoenix can rely on close contact with local officials. Indeed, in the case of Phoenix most village officials are active in the community organization, giving it a direct line to the village hall, including the offices of the mayor and chief of police. On this level, relationships resemble those in rural communities rather than Chicago. Even in Chicago Heights with a population of 37,000, community organizers can at least be assured an open dialogue with city decisionmakers, a luxury coveted by Chicago organizers.

Access to schools for community organizations highlights another advantage the suburbs have over Chicago. CAP's Washington works

closely with schools in two of the poorest sections of Chicago Heights. He
has earned the respect and admiration of the school principals and district
administrations, and his community committee is able to use the schools'
facilities. According to Whitaker, "Even in the larger suburbs you have a
self-contained community that enables you to pull together resources that
Chicago is unable to give up." One long-standing frustration of community leaders in Chicago is the extensive system of public schools that are
under most guidelines closed to the communities after school hours and
during the summer. In most suburbs, community organizers who are
willing to develop the confidence and respect of school administrators will
find the facilities open to them, according to Whitaker.

The relationship that Washington's Chicago Heights Community Committee has fostered with the local schools is seen at the Charles E. Gavin
elementary school on the depressed east side of Chicago Heights. The
school sits in the shadow of the Cook County Housing Authority projects
and the rusting hulks of a dying manufacturing base. Almost 98 percent of
the children come from families on some type of welfare and most are
from single-parent families. The school is unable to meet all the needs of
the 400 children and many rely on community help. Principal Yvonne
Robinson said, "One of the strengths of our school is to bring in
community organizing." The services Washington's organization provides

Ford Heights: on the frontier

"Ford Heights is one of the most incredible challenges we are facing
today," according to Chicago Area Project Executive Director David
Whitaker. "You don't have one particular issue; instead there is a whole full
range of issues to organize around. So where do you start? How do you
begin to attract people when their most pressing problems are on a day-to-
day surviving level?"

Community organizers like Whitaker admit they have few answers. He is
not leading the charge into Ford Heights armed with a battery of prede-
signed programs and rock-solid answers. A Chicago Area Project (CAP)
affiliate is quietly setting up a community center with no pat answers, no
precedents and no promises.

Ford Heights gained notoriety in 1987 when a Roosevelt University
study named the community of 5,300 the poorest suburb in the nation. Per
capita income stands at $4,500, a full $2,000 below fellow south-suburban
community Robbins, which was named 10th poorest in the nation. Illinois'
per capita income is $16,000. Unemployment in Ford Heights is estimated
at around 60 percent.

The Chicago Heights Community Committee, an active CAP branch
that neighbors Ford Heights, is three months away from opening up what it

run the gamut from tutoring students after school to providing organized activities in the summer.

On the other side of Chicago Heights lies Beacon Hill elementary school. Though located in Chicago Heights, it is part of a different school district from Gavin school (highlighting the patchwork nature of suburban government). While Beacon Hill is a community with all the suburban trappings — wide, meandering streets, lawns and ranch-style homes — it is obvious that this surburban dream has gone awry. An estimated 35 percent of the substandard houses stand vacant, stripped of even the aluminum siding. There is no community center and no park in the neighborhood. "We simply can't close our doors to the community," said Principal Ellen Currins. In the summer, the CAP community committee has use of the cafeteria, gymnasium and playground. The organization also runs a hot breakfast and lunch program for the community during the summer months for children and their parents.

One disadvantage Whitaker sees to organizing in the suburbs is the isolated nature of many lower-income areas. "In Chicago there are resources we have learned to rely on, foundations and corporations for example. In an area like Ford Heights, for example, it's difficult because nobody knows about it." The pockets of poverty outside the city limits of Chicago may call for a different approach because of their isolation.

---

hopes will be a model center in the devastated community. The Chicago Heights group was able to secure a vacant Cook County Housing Authority building on the south end of Ford Heights. Thornal Washington, director of the community committee, said his organization's goal is to serve only the small cluster of housing authority buildings near the new center. Washington will focus on the needs of elementary children and their single-parent mothers, who almost exclusively comprise the housing project's population.

Donald Passmore, one of Washington's assistants, will lead the project in its initial stages. Passmore was instrumental in starting up the community committee's site in the Beacon Hill neighborhood of Chicago Heights. A burly, pragmatic and tough organizer, he refuses to be fazed by even the Third World appearance of Ford Heights. He matter-of-factly discussed the first step: to clean up the rubble-strewn lot that comprises the project's grounds and paint over the gang graffiti. An organization must create an environment where people have respect for their surroundings before anything else can occur, Passmore believes.

Whitaker describes this project as the cutting edge of community organizing. There are no past experiences to draw upon, no precedents, he asserts. "We're on the frontier."

But the south suburbs are by no means exclusively comprised of ravaged communities. Intermixed with the poorest suburbs in the nation are many more upper- and middle-class neighborhoods of both whites and blacks. For these communities where local needs are already being met, suburban organizing with a regional focus may be the shape of things to come. The impetus for community organizing in the south suburbs is the exact opposite of that in larger cities, according to the Rev. Larry A. McClellan. McClellan, currently senior pastor at St. Paul Community Church in Homewood and former village president of Park Forest, said the central task for organizers in Chicago is to empower local neighborhoods and community leaders. In contrast, he argues that this is unnecessary in the suburban setting. McClellan believes the various local suburban governments serve as the power base for neighborhoods. What community organizers need to do instead is "systematically develop a regional capacity to deal with public issues" — in other words, cross municipal boundaries to address a common goal not for one community, but rather for the benefit of the south suburban region as a whole.

The economic downturn that occurred as heavy industry left the region spurred a flurry of regional organizations. The South Suburban Mayors and Managers Association, the South Suburban Housing Center, the South Suburban Heritage Association and the South Suburban Action Conference grew out of this trend, McClellan said. All attempt to address problems common throughout the region through intergovernmental cooperation. Therefore, the south suburbs are today addressing problems both through community organizing strictly on the local level and also through regional approaches.

The case of I-Watch and the village of Phoenix, though, demonstrates the difficulty in organizing beyond real and unofficial barriers between communities. Phoenix does not exist in a vaccuum. Bordering the all-black village of 3,000 are two larger communities. To the east is South Holland, a mostly white village of 25,000, and to the south and west is Harvey, a mostly black and industry-based city of 36,000. The problems of Harvey, especially crime, are also the problems of Phoenix, and the two communities share many common bonds. But the only contact most Phoenix residents have with South Holland is the fact that their children are sent to a South Holland school district. Racially, economically and socially, the differences between South Holland and Phoenix are striking. Other than the school, the communities of Phoenix and South Holland might as well be divided by a chasm a hundred miles wide. It is ironic that a number of neighborhoods in South Holland are for the first time organizing crime watch groups with programs and goals similar to I-Watch. Yet there is no communication between the two. In the south suburbs, political boundaries can serve as cultural and economic boundaries as well. Community organizers reaching beyond such boundaries must grapple with this issue first.

This problem is, of course, not unique in the suburban setting. Community organizers in Chicago must also deal with neighborhoods split along racial and economic lines. But the problem can be exacerbated in the suburbs by the sheer number of town and city governments and the wide-ranging types of neighborhoods that make up the communities. Within the diversity of the suburban setting, people organize to make life better in their villages and neighborhoods. But they can be of little help to each other unless they have the networks to share ideas and resources.

While CAP and I-Watch are concerned with providing services on a local level, a number of organizations have taken McClellan's regional approach. The South Suburban Action Conference (SSAC), a coalition of 27 churches, has made the rehabilitation and resale of vacant homes to first-time, low- income buyers one of the organization's top priorities. A conservative estimate places the number of abandoned homes in the south suburbs at 3,000. Not only do these houses add up to an eyesore, they lower property values and neighborhood morale and provide a perfect infrastructure for illegal activity.

Working with area banks, local governments and the state, SSAC is the only community organization addressing housing in the south suburbs on such a wide scale. In cooperation with the Romeoville Housing Redevelopment Commission, SSAC recently gained a $200,000 Illinois Housing Development Authority loan. The loan is enabling SSAC to rehabilitate houses in Sauk Village, Markham and Harvey and to search out low-income buyers. Five area banks have committed low-cost mortgage funds ranging from $80,000 to $500,000.

The careful sidestepping to accommodate the numerous local governments in the south suburbs makes an operation on the scale of SSAC difficult. Some local neighborhood improvement groups quietly combat the movement of low-income and minority home buyers. In the south suburbs as in Chicago, race defines many delicate maneuverings. SSAC is committed to fair and open housing in the region, but combating prejudice based on property values has never been a great success of community organizing. Also, vacant homes are appearing faster than they can be labeled and targeted for rehabilitation. Entire communities, including the more blighted areas, remain untouched by SSAC's efforts.

The challenges are immense. As a community, Phoenix has the institutions to allow Hawkins and his I-Watch group to take on crime in their neighborhood, but in nearby Chicago Heights an east side neighborhood provides a different type of "support." There some of the 6-year-olds come to Gavin Elementary School with monopoly money and pencil shavings in plastic bags to play drug dealer during recess. With drug dealers for role models, the future for many first graders is bleak. Can a handful of CAP organizers working with the school make a dent in the social and economic problems plaguing these communities? Can the south suburbs as a region back them up?

Organizing Downstate: Conflicts and Coalitions

by Cheryl Frank

*'Few applications to restructure debt were
approved in 1986. Almost everyone our age
who bought land ended up in trouble.'*
Chris Foster

Photo courtesy of Illinois Issues

C ommunity organizations have put down roots in the last 15 years in the state's economically troubled farmlands and mid-sized cities. Working out of many traditions, groups representing minorities and low- and middle-income people now wield some power downstate. Increasingly, they're coming forward with demands for basic services, representation and environmental protection in their communities. Their agendas include better health care, lower utility rates, safe and adequate groundwater, help for family farms and civil rights. Intense about their independence and far from agreement on whether or not to back political party candidates, downstate groups are nevertheless joining coalitions to increase their clout with the General Assembly and Congress. And although these groups get advice and support from the Chicago organizing network, they're quick to point out that downstate has a style of its own. Their stories illustrate how organizing plays in places like Champaign, Pembroke, Herrin and Springfield.

In Champaign-Urbana physicians and hospital administrators appear to have eliminated medical expenses that senior citizens elsewhere pay out of their pockets. Hospitals in the Twin Cities also provide a substantial portion of free care for poor people who lack Medicaid or other insurance. Taking a lot of the credit for these accomplishments is an organization called the Champaign County Health Care Consumers. Its organizer, spokesman and director is Michael Doyle, 34, of Urbana. He lives with his wife and three small sons in a modest but pleasant home a few blocks from Carle, Mercy and Burnham hospitals — institutions he has freqently butted heads with.

As a Chicago teenager in the 1960s, Doyle heard stories about organizing from his stepfather, a former Jesuit, who worked with Saul

Cheryl Frank is a reporter for Lee Enterprises Inc. in its Statehouse bureau in Springfield. A community organizer in Champaign-Urbana in the early 1970s, Frank has also worked for state agencies and has been a writer for the *American Bar Association Journal.* "Community Organizing Downstate: Conflicts and Coalitions" was first published in the June 1989 *Illinois Issues.*

Alinsky in The Woodlawn Organization. "I had that orientation back then, growing up," Doyle says. But his first involvement was in the anti-war movement. When that ended in 1975, he came to Champaign-Urbana planning to enter law school and make straight A's. Instead he attended a workshop on low-income health care and caught the organizing fever.

In 1977, while a student in urban planning at the University of Illinois, Doyle helped found Champaign County Health Care Consumers. That same year he attended a training session for organizers held by Heather Booth, founder of the Midwest Academy in Chicago. He was impressed with Booth and her ally, Robert Creamer, founder of the Illinois Public Action Council (IPAC). Doyle's group became an IPAC affiliate in 1978.

Creamer and Doyle both say that until 1980, the Champaign County group was somewhat of an IPAC maverick. Its focus was medical care for the elderly and the poor, while IPAC concentrated on tax relief, lower utility rates and neighborhood preservation. Then health care issues blossomed at the national and state political levels, and IPAC realized that it needed to make more use of Doyle's talents. In 1980 he was hired part time as regional organizing director to groom leaders, develop other IPAC-affiliated groups and define strategy and issues.

Doyle combines old-style, direct action organizing with new-breed, politically atuned coalition building. In Alinsky fashion, Doyle and Health Care Consumers relish embarrassing officials judged by them to have done wrong. Doyle's biggest moments come when people get the most angry, the most excited, when they see headlines saying they have won. He also revels in developing strong community leaders, even when it causes difficulties for him. In 1982 there was a power struggle over the choice of a new director. Doyle sided with the majority instead of the "old guard," many of whom had been personal friends.

Doyle says downstate organizing is different from Chicago's, where the organizing culture is more deep-rooted: "In Chicago there is a stridency that you don't find downstate." But downstate, he adds, has definite pluses: You can get the media interested much more readily; you have better access to the mayor and city council members and state lawmakers. "It takes less to get noticed and win," says Doyle.

In the late 1970s, Health Care Consumers mapped out a strategy to involve the poor, minorities and women in health care issues. One of the group's first actions involved Mercy Hospital in 1979. Health Care Consumers said the hospital was billing Medicaid patients for the difference between its Medicaid reimbursment and what it charged private patients. A meeting with hospital management was called and the press was invited. The hospital president said he had not known about the problem and later blamed computer error. Doyle says the hospital had been aware of the problem long before the meeting. In a matter of days the billing policy was changed. "It blew people out of the water. I'll never forget that Saturday afternoon," says Doyle.

Another victory concerned area hospitals accused of improperly figur-
ing debt write-offs. The federal Hill-Burton law, which provided funds for
new hospital facilities, required certain percentages of low-income people
to be served free or at reduced fees. Health Care Consumers protested that
the requirement was not being met locally. By 1982 all major area
hospitals were exceeding the law's quotas.

A third triumph culminated in a 1987 consent decree signed by Carle
Foundation Hospital, agreeing to accept Medicaid patients from outside
the county. Doyle's group had campaigned for two years on the issue.
Tactics included singing embarrassing versions of Christmas carols,
passing a referendum and attracting media attention. Issues of racism and
discrimination against the poor were raised. "The trick, like playing chess,
is to get your opponent to respond to you," Doyle says.

The hospitals see it differently. Melanie Spain, director of public
relations at Carle Foundation Hospital, acknowledges that Health Care
Consumers "plays an important role," but questions its confrontational
tactics and its refusal to give details on consumer complaints. She also says
the membership lists of area IPAC-affiliated groups overlap considerably
and questions how much grass-roots involvement there really is. To join
you simply pay $5 to an IPAC canvasser, says Spain.

Health Care Consumers is now scrutinizing physicians and dentists in
group practices, such as Carle Clinic, to see if they provide access to
medical and dental care for low-income people. Some health care
providers do not accept Medicaid green cards as payment, Doyle says. His
group is also asking whether cesarean sections are more for the conven-
ience of doctors than for the health of mothers and babies. Another issue is
whether senior citizens and others are released from hospitals too early in
order to hold down medical costs.

Health care also looms large in IPAC's plans. Doyle cohort James
Duffett, 31, who spent five years organizing in Danville on union, public
housing and utility issues, recently moved to Champaign to launch IPAC's
statewide campaign for universal health care. Duffett says, "There's a
major crisis around Medicaid statewide. To me, this is an opportunity for
doing something about it."

About 90 miles north of Champaign-Urbana and 25 miles east of
Kankakee, a group of black farmers has been organizing around groundwater issues. Living in a 56-square-mile area called Pembroke, these low-
income families take pride in the vegetables they grow and sell. Their
okra, squash, blue-hull and black-eyed peas, greens, tomatoes and water-
melon are in high demand for Cajun and Creole cooking and soul food.

For the last three years, the Pembroke Area Concerned Citizens, a
group of some 60 farm families, has been protesting the depletion and
pollution of the wells they rely on for drinking water for themselves and, in
some cases, for their livestock. Concerned Citizens, which has received
advice from Chicago organizer Shel Trapp of the National Training and

Information Center, has also raised questions about groundwater pollution from migrating pesticides. The danger is immediate and real. Says local leader Rebecca Strong, "You know, we drink the water straight from the ground." Several years ago, six people died from drinking polluted water and others became ill with fever. Now some think the water may be polluted by septic wastes and pesticides, Strong says.

Strong was reared on a Pembroke farm and is one of the founders of the group. She is called "feisty" and "extremely well prepared" by staffers of state Sen. Jerome J. Joyce (D-43, Reddick), who has worked hard to solve the area's water problems. Strong wants to develop Pembroke and preserve it for coming generations, though she knows that she may be fighting a losing battle as more and more young people leave the area.

Pembroke's groundwater problems began in the early 1980s, when Prudential Insurance Company acquired huge tracts of land in the Pembroke area and across the border in Indiana and began using irrigators to pump water for crops. Steve O'Neil, an organizer then working with the Family Farm Organizing Resource Center in St. Paul, Minn., was helping Indiana farmers whose well water was being depleted. He says he got the Pembroke farmers involved because their wells were drying up, too. After a lawsuit by the Indiana farmers, Prudential stopped irrigating in Illinois and cut back in Indiana, but O'Neil says some Pembroke farmers think their wells are still affected by Indiana irrigation. Meanwhile, in Illinois other farmers with fairly large land holdings use irrigators, and it is not just Pembroke farmers who are losing their well water because of it, says O'Neil. During the 1988 drought anyone who owned livestock and did not irrigate was in trouble. O'Neil says the irrigators pump 100,000 gallons of water per day all summer without any restrictions, day and night. Some don't pump on Sunday, however, he says.

Strong agrees that last summer was terrible. "We had dust storms," she says, noting that many trees that used to hold the soil have been destroyed to make room for the irrigators. Says Strong, "People were carrying water in cartons, buckets, empty bleach bottles. People were taking baths in other people's homes. That really brought us all together because a lot of people ran out of water out here, black and white."

Solutions to the depletion problem will not come easily. The work of Concerned Citizens was crucial in passing amendments, effective in September 1987, to the 1983 Water Use Act (P.A. 85-483). These allow soil and water conservation districts to direct the Illinois State Water Survey and the Illinois Department of Agriculture to check homeowners' wells to see if they meet new depth requirements. (Many older "deep" wells do not and quickly go dry from irrigation, causing people to use shallow-water wells, which some say are contaminated and dangerous.) In addition, when wells used for domestic water supply run dry, the soil and water districts can recommend that the Department of Agriculture step in and regulate withdrawals for irrigation.

But implementing the law is stirring controversy. Strong says the rules being written by the Department of Agriculture benefit large landowners and farmers who irrigate. Sen. Joyce tends to agree with that and is trying to solve the problem, says his aide, Pat McGuckin. One option: require irrigators to replenish depleted water or to pay a tax that would be used to upgrade wells as was done in Indiana. Joyce says that he supports irrigation, "but you don't have to be a pig about it."

Department of Agriculture spokesman Mark Randal says his agency tries to balance interests in the rulemaking process. He thinks Concerned Citizens is asking irrigators to pay for replacing their outdated wells. That might not be feasible, Randal says. He notes that the problem of irrigation and shallow well water depletion is "popping up all over the country" and predicts that ways will be found to deal with it. At no time, Randal maintains, have the irrigators taken the water table below 25 feet. Farmers in other areas of the state must dig wells much deeper than that to get water for home use, he points out. Yet a February 1989 report, *Groundwater Quantity Issues*, by the Illinois State Water Plan Task Force, singles out the sandy-soiled Pembroke area as having unique problems for family farms and their well water supply.

In the coal-rich counties of southern Illinois another rural organization, Illinois South, fights for the family farm and watchdogs the coal industry. Last fall the effort to reduce farm foreclosures brought staff members Chris Foster and Kate Duesterberg to Springfield. They were lobbying for a farm-debt mediation bill requiring local lenders to try to negotiate new payment schedules before foreclosing. For the second year the bill passed, but once again Gov. James R. Thompson vetoed it, saying it would only create conflict between debtors and lenders. Community bankers had opposed the bill.

Foster, 40, now of Leesburg, Ind., first got in touch with Illinois South as a farmer in distress. She and her husband, Ed, and their two girls, were living near Benton on a 420-acre farm, all paid for. They grew wheat, soybeans, milo and raised hogs. In 1979, when land values were at their highest, the Fosters purchased 130 acres of adjoining farmland. Their problems began when the price of land dropped in the early 1980s after two back-to-back droughts. Turning to their creditors to reschedule their debts, they got the cold shoulder. The Federal Land Bank and the Farmers Home Administration (FmHA) were the Foster's main creditors and the ones "most unwilling to work with us," says Chris.

That's when she called Illinois South's hotline to get financial advice. Staff at Illinois South helped the Fosters through an ultimately unsuccessful appeal of the FmHA decision not to restructure their debt. The Fosters, who have now lost their farm, say they are typical in that few applications to restructure debt were approved in 1986. Almost everyone their age who bought land ended up in trouble, says Chris. She says the decision to buy was a good one at the time. The land was next to the main farm, and they had relatives to support: "It would have been a good move, if prices had kept right."

Besides backing family farmers, Illinois South advocates strict reclamation laws for strip-mined land and compliance with federal regulations on liability for subsidence damage. It also watchdogs corporate ownership of farmland. Avoiding confrontational tactics, Illinois South focuses on research, education and lobbying at the state and federal levels.

Illinois South was founded in 1974 by David Ostendorf, a United Church of Christ minister, and his wife, Rosalind — "Roz" as she is known. They wanted to educate low- and moderate-income rural people on pocketbook issues. Another founding member was Mike Schechtman. One story has it that David and Mike came up with the idea over a cup of coffee in the student union at the University of Michigan. Schechtman followed the Ostendorfs to southern Illinois where they continued their brainstorming and organizing. "We started in our dining room," Roz recalls.

An offshoot organization is the Carbondale Farmers Market, where truck farmers sell their produce. But Illinois South's most well-known spinoff is the Southern Counties Action Movement (SCAM). Founded in 1976, SCAM serves Williamson, Jackson, Franklin and parts of Johnson and Perry counties. Duesterberg says SCAM borrows more from Alinsky than does Illinois South. A mass membership organization that doesn't shrink from stirring up a fuss, SCAM opposes large utility rate increases. It also supports better rural health care and affordable housing and wants rural development based on self-development projects, such as cooperatives, rather than tourism. Current SCAM project director is Steve Banker, 41.

According to Banker, both SCAM and Illinois South work with IPAC and with Booth's Midwest Academy in Chicago, but they used to be closer than they are now. The turning point came in 1982 when IPAC formed a political action committee and endorsed candidates, including Democrat Neil F. Hartigan, who was running for his first term as attorney general. SCAM and Illinois South refused to back Hartigan because they said he did not lend support to an elected Illinois Commerce Commission, says Banker. There was a confrontation of sorts when Hartigan told SCAM members that he already had their endorsement through IPAC. "That was the last straw," says Banker.

Explains SCAM board member Maryanne Dalzell of Carterville, "We had a serious disagreement with them [IPAC] when it comes to partisan politics." She adds, "We don't believe in supporting candidates." SCAM's membership, now about 1,500 households, is bipartisan. Partisanship could split the organization, she believes.

In addition to IPAC, Illinois South and SCAM organizers have gotten advice from Chicago organizer Trapp and also work with Springfield-based Richard R. Wood, director of Illinois Impact, a public policy program under the general auspices of the Illinois Conference of Churches. The Rev. Wood heads a growing statewide coalition of religious denominations, mostly mainstream Protestant but nonexclusionary in character, and other groups supporting low-income issues such as welfare reform. Its work includes lobbying, educating, analysis and research. Wood likes the Alinsky approach and sees a growing militancy in welfare reform organizing and other issues.

Like IPAC's Doyle, Illinois South's Roz Ostendorf sees differences in style between Chicago and downstate. She recalls telling trainers at a Midwest Academy session that their tactics would not work in rural communities. "We don't need to start with demonstrating at some official's home," Roz says she told the group. "That's not going to get you

From community organizing
to progressive politics

Robert Creamer is an important figure in understanding Illinois organizing networks — and their politics. The Wunderkind of coalition building, Creamer wears a business suit and talks low-key during his many Capitol news conferences. He is executive director of the Illinois Public Action Council (IPAC), a statewide organization that seeks to forge a "progressive" coalition. IPAC draws its members from labor unions, from organizations pushing for peace in Central America, from farmers, from senior citizen and environmental groups and from proponents of utility reform. IPAC believes that the process of coalition building gives these "interest groups" both a stronger voice and a wider perspective on social change. Currently IPAC has 150,000 individual members and 130 organizational affiliates.

Creamer was a cofounder, in 1969, of the Alinsky-styled Citizen Action Program, the alliance of Chicago neighborhood groups that successfully opposed the building of the Crosstown Expressway. But he saw shortcomings in concentrating on local issues and went on to found IPAC in 1974. During the 1970s IPAC worked with existing groups and also tried to establish community organizations around the state, a "cookie cutter" approach that didn't work well, according to organizer and IPAC staffer Mike Doyle.

In 1980 Ronald Reagan's election convinced IPAC to move into electoral politics. It did so in 1982, along with many of its affiliates. Creamer says that IPAC has prospered and will soon control a political action committee rivaling any in the state. He had hoped the progressive coalition would carry Illinois for Michael Dukakis, but the state went narrowly for Bush. Creamer says that in the future IPAC's membership of Chicago and downstate independent voters could "swing" the state to the Democratic column.

anywhere. You would be considered the kooks in the community."

In the state's capital city, the issue was equal representation for minorities and the testing grounds were the courts, city council meetings and the streets. Springfield was the scene of a key voting rights case that transformed its government and its politics. The lawsuit was given final form by a group of Springfield attorneys, as some grass-roots figures claimed they were not given a big enough voice in the legal strategy. Local black politician Frank McNeil, now alderman of the 2nd Ward on the city's east side, spearheaded the lawsuit. The lead attorneys in the voting rights victory were James and Donald Craven, a father and son team from Springfield. The outcome was a January 1987 federal court ruling that Springfield's at-large elections of city commissioners had denied

Shel Trapp: 'Blessed: be the fighters'

Shel Trapp of Chicago, a man who makes many trips downstate and nationally as a consultant and community organizer, tried for seven years to combine his activism with being a Methodist minister. He quit when a pastor told him: "You know, Shel, you keep doing things like that, and you'll never get a suburban church."

He tells of one impatient community group that employed the style of Saul Alinsky, the man whose name is synonymous with community organizing. They hammered a dead rat to a Chicago alderman's door to dramatize demands to rid the neighborhood of the rodents.

"I don't think anybody can say today they are in organizing and not in some shape or form trace their roots to Alinsky," he says. Trapp helps people form "power organizations." The people must decide what the issues are, says Trapp, never the organizer.

A bald, leprechaunish man, Trapp, 53, has been organizing since 1966 and is now staff director for the National Training and Information Center in Chicago. Trapp says that until about 1974, organizing was mostly "a big-city phenomenon, turf-based." Then, he says, something happened; he's not sure why. Community organizing as he knows it hit the small towns, "another unique change since Alinsky."

That change makes it possible to build Chicago-downstate alliances. Trapp says: "Obviously we would like to see organizing develop wherever people are interested in doing it. You've got to have some kind of presence downstate and some kind of support if you are going to get significant legislation passed. I think the passage of the whole 12 percent plan [Illinois Residential Assistance Payment Program allowing people who meet income guidelines to pay only 12 percent of their income on utility bills in winter months] occurred, particularly, because we were able to get support from Southern Counties Action Movement and other groups in Southern Illinois."

representation to its black citizens. As a result of that ruling, McNeil and Ald. Alan Woodson of the 10th Ward on the far southwest side became the first blacks to be elected to city office in Springfield. At the same time, Dewayne Readus, a nonviolent black militant who heads a small but vocal tenants' rights group, began an ongoing debate on the efficacy of that settlement.

In Springfield, the consensus seems to be that the new aldermanic system of electing one representative from each ward has inspired broader participation in city government by all groups. At-large elections favored the city's affluent and professional southwest side at the expense of both whites and blacks living in the northern and eastern sections of town.

Speaking of his own ward, which is home to many of Springfield's black citizens, McNeil says, "The east side community is now becoming very political. It is looking at issues and it is responding." He feels that's a positive change for an area that has been given a bad name. "In Springfield, when you cross 11th Street, whether you are black or white, you are condemned because you live on the east side. The connotation, the east side, has within it a negativism. You're living in the war zone."

McNeil, 39, from High Point, N.C., started working his precincts in 1980-81 when he ran for the Sangamon County Board. He won. Recalling his entry into politics, McNeil says: "I began what I considered a quest for the low-income, east side residents to be heard on matters of concern to the east side community." He got some support, "but it was like cutting a new path because no one had been as aggressive and upfront as I had been."

That new path was opened by winning the suit, according to former state appellate judge James Craven, the senior member of the Craven team. He believes that civil rights law rather than direct action organizing will be the key to empowering minorities and low-income people in coming years. Direct action organizing, Craven says, is not always effective in fighting entrenched racism. He believes the process of reform is changing: "It has graduated now into a sophisticated use of the legal process, using the Civil Rights Act of the 1960s and amendments to the Voting Rights Act in 1982. Blacks and Hispanics have become sophisticated."

Alinksy, says Craven, convinced the truly disadvantaged that they could do something about their lives. Now the truly disadvantaged are, and should be, turning to the courts, he says. The Craven law office has become something of a national clearinghouse for voting rights cases. Illinois rulings have required Peoria and Danville to change their form of government. Still pending are suits challenging at-large elections in Chicago Heights and in Cook County judicial races.

In the Springfield suit, one of the first in the North, under the 1982 amendments, the plaintiffs had to show that discrimination was the result, but not necessarily the intent, of the commission form of government. The plaintiffs, among them McNeil, said they represented the disenfranchised members of the community. The suit was finally settled with two compromises: Only one alderman instead of two is elected from each ward, and the commissioners have been allowed to stay on the council as nonvoting directors for a period of three years. The Cravens maintain that the compromises, made in consultation with community groups and the plaintiffs, were justified and that the costs of dragging the case out made no sense.

During the 18 months the Springfield suit was going on, Readus, who heads the Hay Homes Tenants' Rights Assocation, led marches and staged demonstrations. A lifelong east side resident, he bitterly opposed the compromise. Readus and his associate, Michael Townsend, a Sangamon State University professor of social work, see it as just one more betrayal of low-income and minority people by members of the white power structure, abetted, they say, by middle-class blacks with a vested interest in cutting political deals. For over a year Readus, who is visually impaired, has been broadcasting his views using language many find offensive, along with his favorite rap music, to listeners in the immediate vicinity over a low-watt FM station. Readus operates the station from his apartment without a license from the Federal Communications Commission.

McNeil says he has problems with people like Readus who preach ideology, just as he has problems with "Buppies," black urban professionals who are interested only in their own personal advancement. He says neither stance does justice to the civil rights struggle. "Those born after 1960 have no sense of what we had to do," says McNeil, who remembers the segregated schools and sit-ins in his hometown. "We tore down the doors for them to advance in the 1980s."

James Craven is also critical of Readus: "Dewayne Readus is a spokesman for a very small group in the black community. I'm not sure they want solutions. You can never ascertain what his gripe is, but this is part of the system. He proves the black community is no more monolithic than the white community."

But Donald Craven is more positive. He says Readus and his supporters spotlighted the lawsuit for months with their demonstrations. "Dewayne's not a thorn in my side," says Donald Craven. "I think that picketing and other events had a good effect." He believes that Readus forces some people to look at problems they'd rather ignore. Among these are safe bus transportation for school children at Hay Homes, day care for mothers living in the project, tenants' rights and allegations of police misconduct.

In 1987 after Gerald Clemons, a mentally ill black man, died after being subdued by the police, the Springfield NAACP and other organizations, including Readus's, demanded an investigation. The police were later exonerated by a grand jury. In that instance there was a sense on the east side that the situation had been mishandled and many residents joined

Readus's demonstration and signed his petitions. "It was wild," Readus remembers, not because he was leading a big demonstration but because people who had been afraid to speak out were doing so.

Readus claims many blacks support his John Hay Homes Tenants' Rights Association, though they do not do so vocally because of fear. That is flatly rejected by McNeil: "Dewayne is on his own crusade. He's Don Quixote himself who lost sight of the goal to change the form of government. Compromise is necessary to govern."

This spring there were allegations in Springfield of police mishandling of situations involving black citizens. The responses of McNeil and Readus contrasted sharply. As of May 3, 1989, Ald. McNeil had introduced an ordinance to create a police-community relations commission to investigate allegations of police misconduct. He was hoping for, but not counting on, police support and said he was getting phone calls from people outside of his ward offering to serve on the commission.

Meanwhile, Readus, who had been denouncing the Springfield police as "death squads," was cited by the Federal Communications Commission on April 6 for operating the FM station without a license. On April 17 he committed civil disobedience by broadcasting illegally. He was not arrested, but faced possible action by the FCC.

Confrontation and negotiation. Dissent and electoral clout. As Springfield's and other downstate stories show, the tensions between these opposites are great and the balance is delicate. All are needed to accomplish democratic social change. Low-income people want to translate court orders, legislation and regulations into tangible results: jobs, education, training, day care, decent housing, participation in government. During the 1970s and 1980s, problems proliferated downstate, forcing frustrated people into action. Their stories were carried in local papers from Rock Island to Danville and from Rockford to Cairo — but there is no cumulative, statewide sense of what these stories add up to. That's for the future to sort out.

Bedrock Democracy:
Community Organizations and
Washington's Civic Legacy

by Christopher Robert Reed

*'We want this powerful infrastructure to grow
because the success of tomorrow's city depends on it.'*
Harold Washington

Photo courtesy of Kenwood-Oakland Community Organization

W ith his characteristic broad and winning smile, Harold Washington performed one of his truly enjoyable duties as chief executive of the nation's third largest city. On this brisk, sunny Tuesday morning in late November 1987, the mayor broke ground for a desperately needed housing development located in the barren landscape of North Kenwood, one of the city's — and the nation's — poorest neighborhoods. It was expected that Washington would return to this site within a year or so to cut the ribbon, signaling the availability of new housing and a fresh start in life for 70 low- and moderate-income families. Illinoisans know this was not to be, for this was the mayor's last public act before he succumbed to a massive heart attack several hours later.

Not lost in this event was the symbolism. It was more than fitting that Harold Washington's final governmental duty involved a community development dream reaching fruition. Washington was not the first to call attention to the city's inadequate housing, nor was he the only proponent of affordable housing. But he was the first to involve community organizations in decisionmaking and building, and that reserves him a place in the history of Chicago.

Washington's policies on federal funding, low- and moderate-income housing and protected manufacturing districts empowered community organizations all over the city. Particularly effective was his empowerment of Chicago's black neighborhoods — neighborhoods that had consistently been denied access to civic necessities: development and employment. They are among the many communities that benefitted from Washington's approach to economic development — an approach that was attacked as " 'redistributionist' and economically counterproductive by the city's business establishment and daily media," according to Mark Hornung in *Crain's Chicago Business,* May 1-7, 1989. In considering the many facets of the weighty problem of exclusion, Washington saw that

Associate professor of history at Roosevelt University, Christopher Robert Reed writes extensively on African American organizations and ideas, " 'Bedrock Democracy': Community Organizations and Washington's Civic Legacy" was first published in the July 1989 *Illinois Issues.*

housing developmentment, an urgent need in the neighborhoods, could also generate employment.

The Washington legacy to Chicago extends beyond his political and governmental style. In the civic realm he made a major impact also. His election in 1983 reversed three decades of black civic subservience to joint black and white political domination (see Christopher Reed, "A century of civics and politics: the Afro-Americans of Chicago," *Illinois Issues*, July 1987). Responsive to the forces that produced his victory, Washington used his power as mayor to magnify the importance of community groups and their constituents. He did this by making them partners in the process of economic development, a role previously denied to Chicago's neighborhoods, especially its black neighborhoods. By doing this he guaranteed that participation in city government would result in true empowerment. This is the core of Harold Washington's civic legacy, 1983-1987.

The nature of this empowerment is most obvious in the neighborhood-downtown relationship. During Mayor Richard J. Daley's years, the tendency to respond to market signals had resulted in a downtown-first ideology that remained in force after his death. Economic development was a sancrosanct bastion open only to corporate leaders in banking, real estate and construction along with Democratic party stalwarts, as Gregory D. Squires et al. point out in *Race, Class and the Response to Urban Decline*. Those neighborhood organizations that enjoyed access to federal Community Development Block Grant (CDBG) funds had to be content with what was left after the funds had been used for other purposes. School budget deficits were erased. Big developers benefitted. All this violated federal guidelines mandating that the funds be used to help economically deprived neighborhoods.

Reversing that trend, Washington pushed for democracy in the political economy. "Bedrock democracy" was the term he used for it in a 1984 address in which he announced that for the first time in the history of Chicago over 600 neighborhood organizations had taken part in planning the city budget. In the same speech he said that his attention to the neighborhoods was "as fundamental a reform in city government" as his success in passing the freedom of information act.

As mayor, Washington fostered a shared economic linkage between the neighborhoods and downtown that redistributed the city's resources. He saw to it that the all-important CDBG funds were spent in conformance with federal guidelines in the city's neediest neighborhoods. Some of those neighborhoods had never before had access to government funds, notes Hornung in the May 1-7 issue of *Crain's*.

With federal housing money drying up during his administration, Washington also encouraged a public/private partnership in financing low- and moderate- income housing. The Chicago Housing Partnership, established in 1984, enabled city banks and corporate funders to work with the Chicago Housing Department and nonprofit developers. The partnership leveraged the resources of the private sector to the city's neighborhoods (see "Low-income housing without fed's largess," *Illinois Issues*, October 1987). Currently, it has generated 1,800 units of affordable housing, according to Hornung in *Crain's Chicago Business*, May 15-21, 1989.

Indeed, housing was a major theme of Washington's speeches throughout his tenure as mayor. In his first State of the City address to the civic-minded League of Women Voters in 1984 he presented the problem: "If you could ride with me one of these days while I drive through the neighborhoods, you'd be shocked at the shape our housing is in. There are more than a million houses and apartments in Chicago, and 149,000 of them are substandard. We have been losing 6,000 places to live a year, year in and year out for two decades." Washington came back to the subject again and again, giving the number of units built or rehabbed — 12,000 by October 1984, 18,000 by April 1986.

The Washington dream of bedrock democracy was implemented through the city's network of community groups. Over years of struggle these groups had developed an indigenous leadership and an involved constituency. They provided services such as day care, parenting classes, health maintenance and tutoring, and they had also spun off nonprofit corporations for economic development. Thus Washington did not have to create new leaders or a new infrastructure to bring the city's resources to its neighborhoods. Both were already in place. "We all know the strength of the grass-roots leadership because our election was based on it," Washington said in his inaugural speech. "We want this powerful infrastructure to grow because the success of tomorrow's city depends on it."

That infrastructure is made up of hundreds of community organizations. Some of the oldest and most active are in the neighborhoods on the city's predominantly black south and west sides. These are a few of their stories.

On the city's south side, just south of the University of Chicago and separated from the lake by Jackson Park, is the community of East Woodlawn. It is served by The Woodlawn Organization (TWO), founded in 1960. TWO was anchored in the commitment of its founding organizer Saul Alinsky to community involvement and in a dream of empowerment of the kind that Harold Washington's ascension to power brought. TWO is currently headed by Lauren E. Allen, who serves as president and executive director. Young, energetic, intelligent and battle-scarred after almost a decade of service within TWO's hierarchy, she notes how consistently TWO has kept to its original goal of citizen involvement. TWO's basic unit of organization still remains the block club. Allen says, "We are mainly an advocacy group which represents the low- and moderate-income people of Woodlawn." Regular meetings of TWO's various committees deal with problems that the neighborhood residents think are important. They cover matters ranging from crime prevention to education, from alcohol dependency to parenting, from housing to employment.

The Washington years brought a substantive change in the relationship that TWO had experienced with successive city governments since 1960. Confrontation during Mayor Richard J. Daley's administration was followed by a promise of increased community input by Mayor Jane Byrne. But because of political pressures she was either unable or unwilling to carry her commitment to fruition. Allen describes the change after Washington took office as one in which cooperation and active partnership replaced confrontation. She recalls that "partnership had real meaning under Harold Washington. Just by picking up the telephone you felt that your voice was going to be heard on important economic matters." She adds, "We were able to sit at the negotiating table as equals."

Washington could also be relied on to keep City Hall commitments pre-dating his administration, such as the removal of the station terminus of the Jackson Park elevated line at 63rd Street and Jackson Park. A remnant of the Columbian Exposition of 1893, it had become an obsolete eyesore by the 1980s. Allen feels that in spite of tremendous opposition from powerful downtown interests, Washington kept the pledge to remove the structure — much to the neighborhood's and TWO's delight. The Washington administration also strengthened the downtown-neighborhood linkage by instituting a Neighborhood Land Use Task Force during the winter of 1984-1985. The task force brought together affluent opponents of lakefront overcrowding, community groups that wanted houses to be built on the thousands of vacant lots dotting the city, and beautification advocates of Chicago's splendid boulevard system.

TWO's successes in economic development are best seen in its Woodlawn Garden and Jackson Park Terrace apartments. It opened the former in the 1970s with 500 housing units for low-income families and administered them until several years ago. By 1975, TWO had secured a combination of private and public funding and was able to develop the Jackson Park Terrace Apartments, its most ambitious housing endeavor. An eye-catching architectural blend of townhouses and a high rise, the apartments face spacious and verdant Jackson Park along the south shore of the lake. Residents were drawn from East Woodlawn as well as adjacent communities and represented a mix of moderate- and low-income families. During the Washington years TWO built additional units adjoining the Jackson Park Terrace development. These include a mix of housing for the elderly and for low-, moderate- and middle-income residents. Presently, TWO can boast of having developed over 1,400 housing units in the last 20 years, representing over $40 million in capital investment.

Along the lake to the north of East Woodlawn but separated from it by well-to-do Hyde Park, lie the impoverished North Kenwood and Oakland communities, home to the Kenwood Oakland Community Organization

(KOCO). With 43 percent of its land base vacant, 68 percent of its families headed by single parents, and a median income level of $7,000, KOCO struggles against immeasurable odds. Founded in 1965 during the period of civil rights confrontation and self-help planning, it has struggled to improve the quality of life for community residents — usually without needed local governmental support. KOCO's president and executive director is Robert L. Lucas, a civil rights activist who joined the organization in 1969 and assumed his current position in 1975.

KOCO seeks to involve residents of North Kenwood-Oakland in the many aspects of housing revitalization. These include housing rehabilitation and summer inspections of heating systems to prevent unheated apartments in winter, as well as organizing tenant councils and locating financial resources for new housing units, such as the Woodlawn Village Townhouses. The staff and members of KOCO can also be found promoting economic development among local businesspeople, generating job-training programs and working to prevent juvenile delinquency.

As a World War II veteran who fought for democracy and empowerment abroad while he served in Europe, Lucas envisioned a better future for African Americans after the war. Instead, difficulties with the city government, then under the control of Mayor Richard J. Daley's Democratic machine, became the norm. For example, during the 1960s and 1970s Daley refused to allow federally mandated community development advisory committees to be established. As a result, the needed mechanism for funding housing was crippled. Under succeeding mayors Michael A. Bilandic and Jane Byrne, participatory democracy appeared to be served with the establishment of advisory committees on the spending of federal funds. This was done, however, without any semblance of meaningful participation leading to control over actual spending.

Lucas recalls that the Washington era brought in a new standard for the government-community organization relationship. He said that "when Mayor Washington turned over the first spade of dirt to break ground last November [1987] for KOCO's 70 townhouses, he launched the first private housing construction that our community had seen in decades. I think that it is significant that Harold gave this new life to our community on the same day that his life tragically ended."

Even after Washington's election, the struggle against exclusion continued. Lucas remembers how in 1984 KOCO threatened to sit-in at the office of the City Council's Finance Committee, headed by Ald. Edward Burke, to protest Burke's deliberate interference with the distribution of federally mandated Community Development Block Grant funds to underprivileged neighborhoods. This was a manifestation of Council Wars at its worst.

But Washington, another war veteran, won the day. Lucas says that "government under Harold Washington was very open. I remember going down to City Hall on Saturdays and getting involved in governance.

Harold did more than make you feel as though you were just part of the process. You *were*, in fact, a part."

The recently completed townhouses shine as beacons in Kenwood-Oakland's bleak landscape, showing what can be done to improve the community. KOCO is now planning to build a commercial shopping strip on its southern perimeter along 47th Street to revitalize the neighborhood. Perhaps KOCO's proudest accomplishment is its having produced 350 completed housing units over the last 14 years, 70 of which are new townhouses and the remainder rehabilitations.

Due west of the Loop is one of the city's oldest communities, Near West, and adjacent to it, East Garfield Park. This is the area in which the Midwest Community Council has been active for several decades. Midwest was originally formed in 1946 by white businessmen when the area was the scene of several thriving commercial strips, especially along the two miles on west Madison Street from the Chicago Stadium (home to the Bulls and the Blackhawks) to spacious Garfield Park. The two decades following Midwest's founding brought a retreat of heavy and light manufacturing from the area and subsequent unemployment, racial change, political dependency and all the ills of urban blight that adversely affect human beings and neighborhoods.

Since the rioting in 1968, the Midwest Community Council has been led by community activist and former staff member Nancy B. Jefferson. She now serves as chief executive officer and president of the organization. As with TWO, the heart of the Midwest Community Council is its network of block clubs that crisscrosses the greater west side, even beyond the council's service area. Jefferson, whose compassion and matronly bearing have earned her the sobriquet of the area's "Mother Theresa," envisions Midwest's task as "Making the Westside the Bestside." This also serves as the group's slogan and battle cry when confronting widespread crime, environmental problems, unwholesome conditions in the city's park system, education issues or citizens' lethargy. Adding to Jefferson's magnetism is her active participation on the city's police board and other agencies. She has developed a reputation among the people of Chicago as a person who gets things done, even at the sacrifice of her own health.

Realizing that solving housing needs would also impact positively on the area's crushing unemployment problem, Midwest has sought to combine housing and jobs whenever possible. Sometimes this has required direct action, such as was taken in the mid-1980s. Executive director Joseph L. Banks, who has been working with Jefferson since 1976, recalls that "Unfortunately, it had become a historical fact that blacks usually found themselves looking through the fences of construction projects, seeing other people from outside their community working and earning a living while they remained unemployed." In response to this situation, scores of able-bodied, ambitious men gathered under the Midwest banner to seek work at various construction sites throughout the community. The men arrived at one site at 4 a.m., laden with tools and ready to work. Banks says that the construction company's managers called the police, but what they ecountered were not troublemakers but citizens "ready to work, not armed to fight." Negotiations ensued on the spot, and part of the group was employed.

Beyond direct action such as the construction site picketing by its Thursday Night Men's Task Force, Midwest has completed projects to improve housing owned or rented by senior citizens. It is now making plans for new housing construction for low- and moderate- income families in the western end of Near West within a half mile of the proposed controversial Chicago Bears stadium site. Banks explains with a profound sense of gratitude that "Washington empowered us. Who would imagine before Washington's administration that the owner of the Chicago Stadium would call Midwest's president Nancy B. Jefferson directly regarding development of the area surrounding the stadium?"

While the Midwest Community Council supported stadium development as an overall benefit that would revitalize the area, a group of west-side clergy in the area surrounding the Chicago Stadium arrived at a different assessment. These clergy, black and white, Protestant and Catholic, formed the Interfaith Organizing Project (IOP) in 1985. Their purpose was to challenge uncontrolled, exploitative real estate development in several square miles immediately surrounding the medical complex that encompasses Cook County, University of Illinois Research and Rush-Presbyterian hospitals. The medical complex is adjacent to the Chicago Stadium. Once the owners of the Chicago Bears showed an interest in some of the same land, IOP sprang into action.

Where Midwest and Mayor Washington saw development with neighborhood benefit in the area next to the stadium, IOP, according to group spokesman Ed Shurna, saw "displacement after years of deliberate neglect." At this point, he says, IOP committed itself to fight against "deconcentration of the poor for the benefit of the rich" and even took its displeasure to the doors of the Bears' owner. Despite a reputation of being anti-development, IOP was never anti-development, only anti-exploitation, according to Shurna. It is now looking over its own plans for developing the area around the Chicago stadium but is having difficulty in securing funding from either private or public sources.

Serving the West Garfield Park and East Austin communities directly west of East Garfield Park is Bethel New Life, Inc. and the Bethel New Life Community Development Organization under the directorship of Mary L. Nelson. Bethel was founded in April 1979 by Nelson, a former civil rights activist and the daughter of Lutheran missionaries. This white, middle-aged woman has infused religious energy and strength into economically depressed, physically blighted, all-black West Garfield. A quote from Scriptures (Matthew 19:26) displayed in a Bethel publication shows where the group believes it finds its source of strength and confidence: "He looked straight at them and answered, 'This is impossible to man, but for God, everything is possible.'"

Bethel's programs for recycling, holistic health care, family and group counseling, adult day care, infant mortality reduction, and employment and training complement its comprehensive housing program. Jimmy and Rosalynn Carter were hosted by Bethel in the summer of 1986. The former president and first lady lived on the city's west side and worked in a group of 120 volunteers. Their job was to build four houses in one week from scratch. Another project completed in 1985-1986 had Bethel renovating a former public school building on west Madison Street and converting it into an apartment-education complex.

Political change at City Hall in 1983 made a difference in Bethel's activities. Nelson says that once Washington came into office, "he opened the doors to the corporate world [for financing] and we didn't have to go begging anymore." She adds, "He brought us to the bargaining table where before there had just been corporate and political types." Quoted in the neighborhood-oriented publication, *One City*, in 1988, Nelson assessed the Washington years: ". . . . here was a public servant who was indeed committed to neighborhoods, who instructed the departments of government [to include us in] decision-making. . . . Those of us who in the 1960s had to struggle, to protest and to reject so many things now had to change gears."

Through Bethel's commitment to man and God, new townhouses were built, apartments rehabbed in previously abandoned "three flats" and affordable modules constructed as community showpieces. Even a former luxury hotel, the Guyon, has been restored with its 114 housing units and eight storefronts. The mix in several of these units, interestingly enough, is not only low- and moderate-income but includes some middle-income residents also.

Very similar in the scope of its myriad activities to TWO, Bethel can be credited with completing 400 housing units since its formation in April 1979. Impressively, an additional 350 are on the drawing boards. To date, Bethel has completed work with a value of $37 million, proving that the organization's motto, "Development without Displacement," is possible.

The Washington legacy of civic empowerment is in danger at present for several reasons. In the area of economic development, the funds that Washington distributed so fairly to neighborhoods are drying up as the federal government continues its budgetary retrenchment. Funding from the private sector is of great importance in sustaining the civic housing thrust, but the private sector alone will never solve the city's or the nation's housing problem. In the area of politics, after the recent election of Richard M. Daley as Chicago's mayor, many neighborhood groups fear that the downtown economic focus of Daley the Elder will be instituted again, much to the detriment of Harold Washington's legacy of "bedrock democracy." Chicago's neighborhoods are waiting to see what he does.

Photo by Jon Randolph

Danny Solis, executive director of United Neighborhood Organization (UNO) of Chicago, explains UNO's education proposal to parents and teachers at Youngman School in Pilsen. UNO and other community groups helped shape Chicago's decentralized school reform.

Photo courtesy Kankakee Journal

Rebecca Strong with her son Adam points at an irrigation rig — the cause, she says, of the drying up of Pembroke Township residential wells during the 1988 drought.

Photo courtesy Developing Communities Project

Loretta Augustine, vice president of Developing Communities Project (right) discusses job training needs with Mayor Harold Washington (center) and Maria Cerda (left) at the new Intake Center for the Mayor's Office of Employment and Training.

Photo by Thom Clark

David Del Valle, an organizer for the Northwest Community Organization (NCO) holds the sign that Commonwealth Edison used to mark PCB clean-up sites. NCO designed and posted its own bilingual signs for the sites. At right is NCO leader Faith Urrutia.

Photo courtesy Illinois Public Action Council

Photo courtesy National Training and Information Center

Robert Creamer, executive director of the Illinois Public Action Council, headquartered in Chicago with offices in Champaign, Edwardsville, Rock Island and Rockford.

Shel Trapp, staff director for the National Training and Information Center in Chicago. Trapp has been a consultant for community organizations downstate.

Photo by Paul Beaty

Chicago Area Project works closely with the school district in this Chicago Heights neighborhood of Beacon Hill, where one-third of the suburban, ranch-style houses stand vacant.

Photo by Paul L. Merideth

Heather Booth and Chicago civil rights leader Al Raby enjoy a light-hearted moment at a panel discussion held at Roosevelt University November 14, 1988. This was Raby's last public appearance. He died November 23 at the age of 55.

Photo courtesy Innerfaith Organizing Project

Members of the Innerfaith Organizing Project from Chicago's Near West community picket the Winnetka residence of Chicago Bears' president Michael McCaskey. They were protesting development plans for the proposed, controversial Bears' Stadium in their neighborhood.

From Tom Gaudette:
Good Stories and Hard Wisdom

Excerpts from an Interview

*'They all agree on what they're going to do and they're
angry. And they just stand up and say, "Don't
you push me around once more." That's organizing.'*
Tom Gaudette

T rained by Saul Alinsky, community organizer Tom Gaudette founded the Northwest Community Organization in 1961 and the Organization for a Better Austin in 1966. At one point in the mid-1960s a coalition of community groups that he helped organize spanned Chicago, stretching from the suburbs east to the Kennedy Expressway. Gaudette did his organizing with the help of his wife, Kay, and the participation of their seven children. He trained a generation of community organizers, some still working in Chicago and the Midwest, others in Oakland, Seattle, New Orleans. He also trained organizers in Hong Kong, Singapore and Manila. In 1972 Gaudette became head of the Mid America Institute for Community Development, a training and consulting organization. The institute has regional affiliates in the Northeast, the South, and on the West Coast, each serving several community organizations.

The Gaudettes still live in their house in Beverly, a favorite gathering place for Chicago's community organizers in the 1960s and early '70s. This interview took place there on July 15, 1989, a day after the 50th anniversary of the founding of the Back of the Yards Neighborhood Council by Saul Alinsky and Joseph Meegan. The interview is part of a larger oral history tape recording made by Gaudette for *Illinois Issues*. Peg Knoepfle and Tom Gaudette are the two speakers, but the voices are many. That is because Gaudette often turns his stories of organizing into dramatic dialogues — which indeed they are.

TG: This week — and I have the first agenda down in the basement of the Back of the Yards — and they're out there right now in California celebrating the 50 years. My only question is, "Did they invite Joe Meegan?"

PK: He's still in Chicago?

TG: Oh, yeah. Fifty years. That's why sometimes I get mad when different people say they disagree with Saul. Of course everybody disagreed with Saul.
    "But the methods — "

I said, "He had no methods."

If you knew who Saul was, he was a conversationalist.

"Don't you want to get people involved in the decisions affecting their lives?"

"Oh yeah?"

That's all he was looking for.

"Aren't you interested? Isn't that exciting that all kinds of people get involved in the damned decisions that affect their lives and straighten out these corrupt politicians?"

It was his method. Now the way to do it was to get enough people together. They all agree on what they're going to do and they're angry. And they just stand up and say, "Don't you push me around once more." That's organizing. So he looked for people that were angry, that said, "I'm sick and tired of whatever." The air, the earth, the water, the slum housing, or sexism, whatever it is.

He'd say, "Come on. I've got an idea."

He'd suck you in. We used to call him — he was like a vacuum cleaner. He'd say, "Come here. Wait till you hear this one." And he was so exciting and so funny. He was the funniest human being. He was funny.

PK: And how did he suck you in?

TG: Kay and I were married, living in Chatham. We got married in 1953. Organizing to me is so natural, so I don't understand a lot of the struggle people have. It's just the way you do things. I was a pilot in the Second World War, and all that kind of stuff just falls in line. So we were in Chatham, a beautiful community. I'm from Boston. Kay's from Chicago. She grew up about a mile from where that was.

A bunch of street kids came in. Now they call them gangs. They came into the neighborhood and they started raising trouble. I said, "That's bullshit." I rounded up some of the biggest, toughest guys you could find — and women — and said, "Come on in." They didn't come in.

And I said, "Come on. Come on.". . .

PK: And this was in Chatham?

TG: Chatham. Which is 79th, 87th, east of the Dan Ryan. We began to meet some beautiful people. Black, white, a lot of politicians. I think of people like Mahalia Jackson, who was living next door to us, Diana Washington, a great woman; Josh White, the folk singer, George Leighton, the lawyer. These were all the neighbors.

PK: This was when?

TG: 1953-55-56-57. . . . So three years later, I became the president of the organization. . . .

PK: This was the Chatham Community Council?

TG: Yes. We did stuff. We rezoned the area. I didn't even know what the hell that meant, but it would be a single family house and they would put two families in it — you know, a stairway going up the back.

We said, "Ah, here we go."

So one of the guys worked for City Hall. He said, "You've got to rezone the area." So we involved thousands of people rezoning the area.

The next experience was liquor stores. Many of the young blacks moving into the area said, "This is the problem. This is what we're running away from. These damn taverns, the prostitutes and everything."

So I said, "Let's do something about it."

That's when we got into local option, which the state of Illinois just defeated because they wanted to cut out the taverns around Wrigley Field. So they passed a law in the state that you can't do that anymore.

PK: So now you don't have a local option referendum?

TG: I said, "What the hell is this?"

But we got into local option. I didn't know what it was. We started with one precinct. The people came to the door.

"Mr. Gaudette, would you include my precinct?"

The thing just got bigger and bigger and bigger.

I said, "Oh my God." I didn't know what the hell I was into.

So this famous guy, Lou Silverman, who still lives in Hyde Park, seven-foot-one, came in and every Sunday for about a month, he would tell the people about local option, in which you actually have ballot boxes. And he showed the people how to beat the system. How to watch out for the troublemakers. They put charcoal under their nails and they put an X on the ballet. That's one technique. The other one is, you must put your signature as a watcher on the ballot, so what they do is go ahead and give them out before they [the watchers] get in. There's a whole series of these things. I didn't know all this stuff. The stuff that they were talking about, that we were training for, began to happen. And the people knew what to do. It was marvelous.

People were saying, "Hey you. Officer, arrest him."

There were lots of arrests.

We had our headquarters at Crerer Presbyterian Church in the basement. I had the police commander there, and the City Council lawyer sitting there, in case we had any trouble. We had 19 precincts, 19 different officers. We had walkie talkies.

"This is precinct No. 3 reporting — "

It was like the military. Saul just loved that scene, people with walkie talkies.

"My name is Mildred. Am I Mildred? Who am I?"

It was marvelous. Anything they tried, we were ready.

"Officer, commander, step into that precinct there and arrest that man and bring him over here."

We were covered. We had the law on our side; we had law enforcement on our side. And the nuns at Mercy High School, I remember, five o'clock in the morning, marching down the street with their rosary beads, going to vote. We don't know whether they voted our way or not. I remember Charlie Davis, the blind guy with the dog at his precinct. It's five o'clock in the morning — "Tom, I'm here." Giving out the ballots, the identification.

The liquor drivers — what do you call them? The truck drivers, the Teamsters came after us. So some of the guys, members of the Meatpackers, they showed up. The United Auto Workers and Meatpackers came with their jackets, and we put five in each precinct as our protection. It was the greatest thing you ever saw. And the police were sitting there. They said, "Holy God, are we going to have a fist fight here!"

And we beat them. We beat the taverns. . . .

And the young people. All of a sudden, we had an identity. People began to come to Chatham. Eddie Rosewell, the guy who collects our taxes in the county now, was a kid from the west side, a young precinct captain who came over to Chatham: "Would you help us in Garfield?"

Just think about it. This was 1956-57 . . . .

*   *   *   *   *   *   *

Now the other thing you learn — Saul used to teach that people did things for different reasons. The nuns weren't anti-liquor. They had a reason.

Somebody else, "I'm going to do it because of this great political thing, see." Politics. "We'll show the aldermen."

That's what I began to learn. You've got to find out the reasons. As long as we're all going the same direction, we can all have different reasons. Rather than trying to convince you that I'm right, as long as we're working together for the same goal, your way is your own business. That was what Saul was trying to explain: the difference between an organization and a movement. In a movement, you have to all agree for the same reason. That's slavery, for chrissake. I have a right to have my own reason and you have a right to have yours, as long as we say we're going to go in the same direction. So little things like that, [things] that happened, later became Alinsky's method.

Saul used to say, "You got any more? I can use that."

When he used to write a book. "I've run out of ideas. Give me another one."

He loved to get inside you. "During the war, how old were you?"

"Eighteen."

"Oh my God. When you took the plane up, and were going to bomb — Vienna? — what were you thinking about?" He'd get inside you. "Who did you think about? Did you cry? Were you scared? . . . And the guys you were with, when you were on the plane, when you were up 20,000 feet, what did you talk about? Did you tell jokes?"

And he would pull out of you an experience, which he would use to interpret what he was trying to do in the neighborhood. That's why he said, "You've got to know the person. That takes time."

PK: So you went around a lot and talked to people?

TG: That's all you do, if you think about it. That's what I try to teach the kids today.

"What are you doing in the office? These goddamn computers. What is an organizer doing sitting at a computer — what's Mary's name? What the hell are you putting on a computer?"

"Well, it's a toy."

"You belong out there."

Saul used to say, "When is your first appointment?"

"Pardon?"

"Nine o'clock, you dumb sonofabitch, what are you going to be doing at nine o'clock?"

"Well, a cup of coffee."

"You're fired. What are you going to do at 9:30?"

And he would say, "You've got to have something set up all the time. Who are you going to have lunch with?"

Leadership. Political, business, economic, religious, social — whatever. Have lunch and dinner with them. He said, "You damn Americans." He said, "You just eat to eat." He said, "You know, in other countries, it's a social experience. It takes three hours to eat dinner. That's what you're supposed to be doing. Sit down with someone." He said, "I'll pay for it."

So you call up the politician, alderman or leader or whoever. And that's how you really begin to get the other side of the coin. In other words, meet with people who aren't in the community, who aren't part of the life, but have power.

PK: So you were doing both of those things.

TG: Yeah. That's the balance. If you don't know what the opposition, whatever you want to call it, is saying or thinking, how the hell do you know it's an issue? You make it up. Once you find out there are many people in power who agree with you — bankers, politicians, who won't do it publicly say, "Kick 'em."

PK: And even though you were with a group that was raising a whole lot of Cain, they would want to come and talk with you?

TG: They're jealous. We used to meet in the back of a tavern with one of the aldermen.
"Tom, this is Charlie. I'll be there at 10."
"Ummm."

PK: And he was your enemy?

TG: He would say, "Publicly, I've got to do this."
And many of them are great people. But they have to put on the image. And many of the people today in City Hall — Jesse Madison. I can show you a picture of Jesse Madison down in the basement. He's the head of the park district now. He has a limousine and so forth. Jesse was the vice president of Austin OBA [Organization for a Better Austin]. Jesse — we used to play ping pong in the office. I'd like to see Jesse now.
"What's your name?"
"Jesse, for chrissake —"
And his house was behind the office on Cicero Avenue.
And then Saul would describe what happens when you get power. That was the other thing. That's what I think he was to me. The technique stuff was routine for him. If you play sports or tennis or raise a family, whatever you do — that's what it's about. When you get up every day to make a decision. What am I going to do next? What about your job? Who the hell am I going to interview? Who do I know?" Details.
But Saul knew the whole thing about people and power. Fascinating.
"Who did I put in power? How did they get it? And how do they use it?"
No moral judgment about power — "There are people in power."
"Uh-huh."
"And people in power make decisions about you."
"Okay."
"No judgment now. How did they get the power? Is it legal? Was it elected? Was it taken? Was it money? Influence? How do they use it? What do they do with the power? That's the question."
When I got into the moral situation with [Monsignor] Jack Egan, I said, "Jack, some of our best friends — when you stay around a while, some of your best friends are now in power. Are they any different from the sonofabitches you argued with 20 years ago?"

PK: Are they?

TG: No. Is there somewhere we can get ahead of the game by saying, when we are in power, "Where are the principles? What is it that's going to keep you operating?"

And I said, "You know, Jack, you're down at Notre Dame" — Jack used to be down there. I said, "Give me the alumni of Notre Dame. If I could clean that up, we'd clean up half the problems in the United States." I said, "They're Catholic graduates. What the hell are we teaching them? Now that they're in power, what's new?"

So we used to love that. See, that's the part of it that makes sense. Once I can figure out who's in power — not just names. What's their mother's name? What church do they go to? — because they usually go to church. All that stuff. Then there's something I can do. Without that, they're still the enemy and I'm righteous. How do you win? But I've got to know something about them, how they think, which I can use in the strategy.

You see, Gale Cincotta is a genius at that. She still thinks she knows every living human being in the state of Illinois. I don't care who it is. She'd go, "Bing, bing, bing, bing. And he lives bing, bing, bing. And he goes bing." Just like a computer, the way she'd say that.

"Gale, that's our job."

Oh, she was so good at that . . . .

PK: So you had the Chatham Community Council. And then Saul came to visit you?

TG: Nick Von Hoffman. Fabulous Nick.

PK: What was he like?

TG: You should meet Nick. You'd love him. He's the craziest human being I ever met. He was a master strategist. He had the wildest ideas — the trouble is we had to go do it, see . . . . He was marvelous. Nick was the closest thing to Saul. They used to sit there like this. They were in my office once, they were sitting on the floor, and I'm telling the truth, sitting on the floor.

"That goddamn John Mills. That stupid sonofabitch."

"What are you talking about? Remember Voltaire."

Well, I'm sitting there — "Who's Mills? Who's Voltaire?"

They were taking it out of a history book and debating. They both knew history. Debating Napolean. I said, "Who the hell are these two — " These two minds would just clash. They'd go on for six or seven hours like that. If I had taped that, I could be a millionaire, could have written a book. And they just adored each other. The father/son relationship. They wouldn't admit it.

"Young punk, when I was that age I was doing something."

"That old bastard, you've got to get him out of here."

When I was the leader in Chatham, he [Von Hoffman] used to go to the meetings. Then he'd come back to the house. My house was a hangout because of Kay [Gaudette].

"Tom, that was the dumbest goddamn meeting I've seen in my life. This is what you did wrong."

I said, "What the hell are you doing here? Who are you?"

He was in charge of the Industrial Area Foundation's research. And what he was doing was watching me. I found that out many years later, after they wrote the book — Nick wrote one, Dave Finks wrote one. And Saul — he [Von Hoffman] was checking me out to see if Saul would hire me.

I was a vice president of Admiral Corporation, and I didn't know anything about Alinsky. Who the hell was Alinsky and all this? I didn't know all this stuff.

In 1961, Alinsky called me up: "Tom? Saul."

"Saul who?"

"Saul Alinsky."

"Who the hell are you?"

"I've been watching you work and I'd like to talk to you. Could you come down to the office?"

I said, "I'm not interested, I've got to go to work. I've got to raise a family, now cut the bullshit."

"Can I see you?"

I said, "All right, what the hell." This is in Fink's book.

He said, "What do you do for a living?"

I said, "I work at Admiral Corporation."

"For profit?"

I said, "Yeah."

"Oh shit, one of those. What do you do?"

I said, "Well, I'm in transportation. I take care of conventions and we have two planes. Anything that moves, I'm in charge of."

"Oh. Do you have a pension plan and everything? Retirement?"

"Yeah."

"Oh, that's too bad," he said. "They've got you. How old are you?"

I said, "I'm 38."

"Oh shit. You're pretty old. I was looking for a much younger person." And he said, "You married?"

I said, "Yeah."

He said, "You got kids?"

I said, "Yeah, we've got five kids."

"You're not one of those goddamn Roman Catholics that don't screw around are you?"

I said, "Yeah, I happen to be one of those Roman Catholics."

He said, "I was looking for a much different person. I'm really not interested."

I said, "You sonofabitch. Who do you think you're talking to . . . ?"

"You think you're tough. Pick up the phone and quit your job."

That's what I did. I'd been wanting to do it. It was true, they had you. It was a little more money. Money. Money. I didn't realize — I went home to Kay and she said, "What do you want to do?"

I said, "I don't know."

And she said, "Well, you love the work. Let's get into it. We'll both do it."

I said, "You sure?"

She said, "Yes."

"Okay."

I said, "Okay Saul, let's try it. What do you have in mind?"

He said, "I don't know. This Jack Egan gave me this group up there. Now they're Eastern European people. Polish. You know that."

A really deep analysis.

"What the hell do you want me to do?"

"Go up there and see if you can build an organization."

"Thanks."

That was my training.

He said, "If you get into trouble, call me."

PK: He was here in Chicago then?

TG: So I'd go down to the office, maybe once a week, and tell him what I was doing. And I began to figure out what he was up to. So what I did to Saul was, I turned it around and used it against him. I never answered the phone when he called. I drove him buggy. Because I had no power — but that's the game we were in. So my power was to show how to manipulate him. I did it. I used to drive him bananas.

"This is Mr. Alinsky. I understand you work for me. Do you mind telling me what the hell is going on?"

So he gave us tape recorders. In those days they were the old Dictaphones. So every night, you'd read into this thing. And that's how I did my reports.

PK: And you did your reports that way?

TG: And I'd mail them in to them and they'd type them up and they'd come back. It was so funny, he began — TWO [The Woodlawn Organization] was going on then, OSC [Organization of the Southwest Community] here, and then what I was doing. He had to give us all dictaphones. We were all the same way. We didn't want to talk on the phone. I was the one that made Saul come out of the office . . . .

"No, no, Saul, you come out to the staff meeting and meet the people."

He loved it. His ego. We'd do all kinds of things — "Now when Saul comes, ignore him, and just go about your business." It was a game that was going on.

"Could I have a cup of coffee?"

"Yeah. It's right over there."
One day we locked the office, wouldn't let him in. He loved that, see. He loved to be turned on . . . .

*   *   *   *   *   *   *

I love parties. That's the other thing that's critical to me. I don't think we celebrate enough. We win things, not me, but — you get people in a bar when they've won something? You've got to tape it. Because you think we exaggerate, you ought to hear the people.
"Well, I mean, there were 2,000 people down there. The mayor actually was crying, he was so scared of us."
It's their chance to be on the stage. To perform. And somebody might be drinking too much. Or somebody's lying or somebody's out dancing or singing. But they're celebrating some event. It's exciting. Put on by the community. We don't do enough of that.
I said, "Did you celebrate?"
"Oh God, I was tired and I went home." This is staff.
"Tough. How about the leadership?"
"Oh I understand Mary's having some of her friends over."
"Where is the celebration? Why do you think we have halls and stages and music? I don't know what your style is, but everybody has music, as far as I know."
It was hard. When we did the rezoning there, it was the first big thing we did at NCO [Northwest Community Organization]. There were 1,100 people downtown. We took on Alderman [Thomas E.] Keane and some of the biggies. We won.

PK: What were they trying to do?

TG: Rezone the area, the community. It was funny. The experience I had in Chatham was rezoning. Now here I am back in West Town at a meeting at St. John's with 600 people and I'm trying to take them into the world of organizing.
"What are you here for?"
"The churches hired me." And so forth. "Give me a problem."
"Well what's the use? The whole area's industrial. The goddamn factories are taking over our neighborhood."
 I said, "You can control that."
"No we can't."
"Yes you can."
"What do you mean?"
"Rezone those factories out of here. If this is a residential area, it should be rezoned."
"The alderman said we can't do it."

"Get the sonofabitch over here. I'm telling the truth."
I asked the committee [22 Catholic pastors] to be there. Now I don't know these people. I've got all the clergy sitting behind me. That's my power.

PK: This was one of your first meetings?

TG: I said, "All right. I think it would be good if you'd go to the aldermen. And I want a businessman, a religious, a woman, a kid." I'm organizing, see. "A kid. And someone to represent the PTA."
"I'll represent the PTA."
"What's your name?"
"Mildred."
"That's good."
And we took about 10 people representing interests. And somebody said, "Well, I represent a union."
"Good, get over there."
The first sense of structure — of an organization.

PK: So that was how you began?

TG: Isn't it logical? When you don't know who's there?
"Any businessmen?"
"Yes sir."
"You're the president of a bank? Would you go?"
So when they present themselves as a power structure, the alderman just says, "Holy shit." The bank, the church, PTA. "What's that kid doing here?"
Power.
So they went over there at nine o'clock. They brought back the alderman [Matt Bieszczat], the guy who used to call me "the commie." There he is with a hat, right out of the movies. And the clergy are all sitting there smoking cigars.

PK: Did they know him?

TG: He gave them liquor and food. He took care of them.
I said, "Alderman?"
"What the hell are you doing here?"
"Alderman, I'm running this meeting. Now let me ask you a few questions." I said, "Father Janiak?" Father [Anthony] Janiak was the president of a local neighborhood organization. "Would you run this meeting?" I stepped aside. I walked off the stage and said, "Alderman, is it possible to rezone this area and protect the homes?"
"Where'd you find that out?"

We had him!

And the people said, "That lying bastard."

These were his people. A lot of precinct captains now. Why would he be opposed to protecting the homes? Think. The homes.

"My home. Why would he do it?"

Without saying it, he got brought out. Just like that. That was the issue.

PK: Education?

TG: So I took the people, and he left mad. We booed him out.

"I want 20 people to stay after the meeting and that committee they got together would be helpful. Any other group that's here tonight? VFW [Veterans of Foreign Wars]? That would be great."

"I'm a veteran."

After that, we put together, until about 11 o'clock at night, an idea of how we were going to do this thing. That was probably in February. On May 1, we marched into City Hall with 1,100 people. It's the funniest story.

I got nine buses and I had a blackboard. There were only two of us, me and Craig [Heverly]. Staff.

"Father? What's it like? Your quota's 250."

"Tom, I'm embarrassed. I've got 310 people here. What am I going to do?"

I've got nine buses. Great strategist. I said, "Craig, we're in trouble. There's a church we didn't even count that just called us. He's got 50 people."

So we started sending them downtown because we didn't have any buses. "Take them down there and dump them and come back, quick."

So we had all the people down there, and I had it all documented — you can't believe it when you're on the phone. You've got the blackboard, you know. Quota, 50. "Eighty?" It was doubling.

So we got down there. I got in the car. I said, "Greg you go first and take care of the people. I'll stay here and get them down there." So I get down there, and I remember the City Council was supposed to start at 10 o'clock. I get there at about a quarter of 10. The place was up for grabs. People all over the place — and I have pictures of them.

This big policeman comes up: "What the hell is going on?"

I said, "I work with the Catholic churches on the north side."

"Oh. I've heard about you. What's up?"

"Well, these people are coming down because the factories are trying to take their homes."

"You're kidding."

"Father Janiak — what's your name? Murphy? — this is Lieutenant Murphy."

"Father, I apologize. I didn't know about this. Let me get this cleared up."

He took everybody up to the chambers.

Smart me. I sent the buses back to the parking lot because this is going to take five hours. See I'm an expert. I know how long these things take. I had all the speeches. I couldn't get in, there were so many people. Of course, we invited all the school kids, the nuns, the street gangs, anybody we could find — "Come on."

So the policeman takes me around and I come up to the second floor of the City Council in the back and there's Mayor [Richard J.] Daley right there, and I've got the speeches. And Alderman Keane, the most powerful alderman in the city is up there.

"Ladies and gentlemen, I'd like to move that we approve the plan. All in favor, say aye."

It took 10 minutes.

PK: Is it the plan that you guys wanted?

TG: We didn't have a chance to give the speeches. And everybody's cheering like mad. I'm saying, "Oh my God, I've got the speeches." We won, but we stayed up all night writing these things. I ran downstairs and people were drawing around — "We won!"

It dawned on me. We don't have any buses. I sent the buses back. The same lieutenant comes over.

"What the hell did you screw up now?"

I said, "I sent the buses back."

He said, "You get paid to do this?" He said, "I'll take care of it." I'm telling the truth. He stopped all the CTA buses, emptied them out. "Ladies and gentlemen, this is an emergency. Please, would you step off the bus? Give them back their money."

He lined up CTA buses for us. We took the people back. It was one of those things I got credit for. I didn't know what I was doing, for chrissake.

PK: This was in the early '60s?

TG: 1962. They just love to beat you. And for years after that, people would always say, "Tom, don't forget the time you sent the buses back." So every time we had an action after this, they'd say, "Tom, do you mind if we take care of the buses? You're not too good at that." But it was marvelous. And the other thing is, people began to realize you were a human being and not an expert. That you could screw things up, see.

And Saul used to say, "Always tell the truth. Why do you lie?"

Never tell people that they can win something if you don't think they can. That's bullshit. That's screwed up a lot of people . . . . Figure out how much you can win and be smart. But tell them the truth because tomorrow they're going to ask you the same question. And you come up with the

same answer. That's what respect means. They trust you . . . . Because part
of the thing we do in life is bluff and make all kinds of excuses. That's
what bothers us. When you tell the truth, and you say "I don't know what
to do," you feel good.

And that's how you have a relationship, because they figure, "Well, if
you don't know, how do we — ? Let's figure it out together." . . .

Gale [Cincotta] was famous for that. She'd come in the office, "I've got
an idea."

"Shut up."

It was a great weight off your back. If you think about it, you're equals.
Remember that word? Equals? Rather than one better than the other?

People used to come into the office: "Who's the boss here?"

"We don't know. Depends on what day it is."

That's how you relax.

So. We finished [the NCO demonstration] and we took the people back
to St. John Cantius, and so help me God, I did not arrange it. I was
downtown, I got into a car and drove back, and there was some beer there
and some food. I said, "What's that for?" People wanted a party. This was
3:00 in the afternoon. I said, "What are you talking about?"

"I don't know. The people went out — "

That's the first experience I had, which was the way I became about
having celebrations. So we can talk about it. I mean, "I wrote that speech
and never had a chance to give it." So we made the people get up on the
stage and give the speech right there. I was so excited, I went down to the
office to Saul . . . .

PK: The Northwest Community Organization, that area — what's it like
now?

TG: It's gone crazy with the "ups."

PK: It's been gentrified?

TG: I'm proud of it. Some of these old houses with no bathrooms —
$300,000. I go up there and clip it out of the paper every Sunday. I don't
believe it. I mean, what happened? It's a great place to live. I mean, there's
some architecture there that's just unbelievable. And the restaurants . . . .
But, you know, I can't explain it, how it happened. They say people can't
afford Lincoln Park, so they're moving over here. North Avenue and
Damen, where the Latin Kings used to be. I said, "I'll be damned." I can
show you pictures. Factories that are becoming condos on North Avenue.

Well, there's two problems. What happens to the people that live there?
So I used to try to teach them to negotiate with the ups. Coming in? That's
great. That's good for the neighborhood. But don't let them take it all over.
So instead of sitting there and saying, "You can't come in. You have no

right to live here" — I mean, we're on the wrong side of that one — let's sit down and negotiate . . . . Which means deal with the realtors, the same old powers, and the banks and whoever.

So I went down to Saul's office, and I was telling him about this thing [the successful NCO demonstration]. And I was telling him, "Yeah. The people were moving in — they were so afraid of us."

The marvelous hindsight. We knew all of this was going to happen. Sure.

Saul would just sit there with a big smile, "Tom, you're not permitted to go back to the party."

"What are you talking about?"

"No. Your job is as an organizer. You've got to go back to the office and figure out, now that you've got it, what are you going to do with it tomorrow. And I'd like a written report on that."

"Oh my God. You sonofabitch."

So I go back: "Craig, we're not supposed to be at the party."

He said, "Why don't you quit your job and then we'll get rehired after the party."

That's what we did. "Screw you, I quit."

We stayed at the party and then that night we got the people together.

PK: So they helped?

TG: We figured it out. "What are we going to do tomorrow?"

"Well, Tom, I never wanted to bring this up, but how about —?" Whatever it was.

Those became the leaders. If you had asked me before that day, "Who are the leaders —?" But after that meeting I knew. Just watch the people. A mother with five kids that lived in this house, her husband was a truck driver. But when I saw her in that City Hall chambers with her mob telling them what to do . . . .

People say, "How do you pick leaders? Do you throw darts?"

Watch. Observe. You can feel it. You can smell it. You can taste it . . . . And that became — it was so obvious. So you have a convention, you have an election. Now the big thing is they negotiate. I was trying to teach them how to negotiate, not argue: "Whatever you want, that's fine. But you've got to negotiate with that group over there. Support their campaign so they support you."

PK: And this was during the election of the officers?

TG: I was trying to teach them politics. That was the dumbest idea I ever came up with. Teach the people politics? For chrissake, they're born with it, but they don't know if it's all right to do it. That's the other problem.

"Is it all right if I support that person?"

So I try to give them, if you will, the platform, the authority, the credentials, whatever the word is, to be a human being and participate.

"Tom, we don't have any Puerto Ricans."

PK: This was also a Puerto Rican neighborhood?

TG: . . . . So before every convention, without my doing it, there was a caucus of the different leadership. That was a strange word. Caucus. Representing different leadership. These are ethnic groups now, discussing who's going to be on first, who's going to be on second. It was marvelous. So we went into the convention — I'm still a nut for conventions. A lot of people don't believe in conventions. But when you sit there and there's a thousand people and there's politics going on and you see people walking around the floor, moving. In different languages. They know each other. That's community, which didn't exist before. And they began to know Jose, and Jose knew of Abel, and Abel knew this one. And you just watch.

Saul used to sit there, and he'd cry. He'd say, "Look at that. It works! Isn't it great? Democracy works." He said, "That's the fight. That's democracy at work. And that deToqueville, that sonofabitch from France. I wish he was here now. Because he said it didn't work. He challenged it. And it works. Look at that!" He'd get so excited . . . .

I keep talking about NCO because it was the first one. It's the magic one. And all the differences in nationalities. Well, we did have the Veterans of Foreign Wars in this neighborhood, who would almost be kind of like anti-ethnic. We did have street gangs.

PK: How did you get them in?

TG: I had a guy, Bob Smith, a minister, whose job was to organize the kids. They had their own convention one month before ours. They had their youth convention, in which they set up and had elections and a guest speaker and cut issues.

Crime. "Who's going to protect these little kids? Fifteen, 10 years old. Who's going to protect the women if the police don't? We will."

Drugs. "Suppose we want to get rid of drugs. What do we do? Where do we go?" They made us open up a drug clinic. The kids.

Jobs. "What the hell's the use of going to school?"

But it wasn't a socialist, a social-action person. It wasn't me. It was them getting up and saying, "What's the use of going to school? I can't get a job. You don't want me."

That's different. Then they would come to me at the adults' convention and demand support.

PK: How did the adults feel?

TG: See, they're organized, there's no mob, see. That's the whole point — the difference between a mob and an organization. They had to ask approval to get into the convention. Credentials. They had to have a place to sit. We purposely put them in a certain place. They could get up to the microphone and speak just like anybody else. Just like adults. And they loved it because they had power. When the people all approved whatever it was they wanted, just like adults they cried.

We had people with us — "What happened?"

All of a sudden, here we go. We respect each other. To me that was exciting . . . .

PK: Where was the office?

TG: It was a storefront. Still is. 1109 North Ashland. Right today. You can go in, and I'll show you around. Saul Alinsky's desk. Pictures on the wall. I walk in, and some of the old-timers — "Here he is. Big mouth. Made money on our work and our misery." . . .

There were so many meetings going on, we couldn't cover them. We just couldn't do it — which later became a technique.

PK: What? Holding lots and lots of meetings?

TG: Yes. But don't go. Staff doesn't go. We couldn't go. Sometimes there would be eight meetings going on at the same time. But the thing was, people used to come back to the office, "Tom, sit down. This is what happened." And we would actually strategize.

So I said, "This is stupid. I'm going to be here until dawn. I'll be here all night." I'd get two groups together.

"What did you have at your meeting? Could you help us with ours?"

They would begin to help each other, strategize about what to do — which later became another technique. I did the right thing for the wrong reason. Remember, Saul used to always tell you to do the right thing for the wrong reason. So you've always got to find the wrong reason. That's how people do things. And I just couldn't physically do it. There were only two or three of us. And we had all these huge groups. It was marvelous when I found out that they didn't need us.

So after awhile I didn't go to meetings, and it made people do things for themselves. Naturally. And they began to treat you like an ego by saying, "Tom, we don't need you at the meeting. If something goes wrong, we'll let you know." That became another strategy.

That's what happens with a lot of staff today. They're so conscientious and have a guilt trip. They attend everything. By 10 o'clock that night they don't have the slightest idea what they did that day. It's stupid. When you think about it, if we've done a good job, what the hell do they need us for? . . .

A friend of mine, Mike Soika, a great organizer, was hired by the new socialist mayor up in Milwaukee to deal with economic development. And he had to deal a lot with the community. He said he never realized how you see a neighborhood from a position of power in City Hall. One, you never see the people; you only see staff, who demand things. Two, most of them don't live in the city; they live in the suburbs. And three, they don't represent a damn thing; it's their idea about what the people need. And what they're saying is that people don't have time. That's bullshit. Two, they're stupid. I love that word. "People are stupid. They're ignorant, see? They're not like me."

And he got so mad, he demanded that the mayor not give any money unless these conditions exist: that 100 people show up. And he began to lay down Alinsky's conditions for an organization. The city got so excited that they offered him their job. He refused. Mike's one of those screwed up guys who doesn't like money. He went back to work for Catholic Charities.

PK: And wherebouts is he working today?

TG: In Milwaukee. But he has that balance. I always tell young people, "Go out and get a job with the power structure and the establishment. Then come back." Rather than debate whether I'm right or wrong, which is what we do. I'm prejudiced, I'm an Alinskyite and all that. Go find out what it's like . . . .

    *   *   *   *   *   *   *

TG: You can kind of get out of the way. Did you ever think of that? Most of the time when I was organizing, I just sat in the car. There were enough exciting people in this office — Gale Cincotta, Ruth [Walters], Ray [Deveraux], and all kinds of people. I can show you pictures where we're sitting around a table at one o'clock in the morning drinking beer . . . .

PK: How did you get into doing the Organization for a Better Austin?

TG: I was in NCO and a lot of the churches were doing great stuff, and some of the people from the community of Austin came out and watched us. They used to sit in on our staff meetings. Our staff meetings used to start at night, 10 o'clock at night, and everybody would come in and we'd get it up on the blackboard. And they observed and they liked it. In 1964, they asked me to come out to a meeting of the churches up in Austin. I didn't know where the hell Austin was. I think there were six Catholic and 30 Protestant and three synagogues and some existing organizations and they got together.

I said, "If I come in, here is what I will do. I need three months to analyze the power structure that exists in this community. At the same time, I've got to find staff, people that will work with me. At that point, I'll present a plan, a three-year plan for what we're going to do." I said, "Right now, I can't tell you what we're going to do. I could say we're going to sit here and build an organization and so forth." I said, "It's going to cost you $75,000 a year" or somesuch. Something like that, it's not clear. "And because of my condition" — I'm married, and this time I've got seven kids . . . . I said, "I've got to have money in the bank before I start."

So in 1966, Kay and I and the family went up to Michigan. We always go up to Michigan. And I got a call from Father Harry Renard. In fact he just died this week.

"Tom, this is Father Renard. We just deposited $100,000 in the bank in your name. When can you start?"

I said, "Father, I'll be there Monday." So that's when I started.

PK: How do you walk into a community and figure out the power structure?

TG: You of all people! Read the newspaper. The first place I go is — "What newspaper do you read?" They had a neighborhood newspaper. There were two women. I said, "Can I go back five years?" They gave me newspapers. And I said, "What names show up? What organizations keep jumping at you? What activities are going on? What businessmen? Who takes out ads?" Just go through the paper. And after about three or four years — bingo! I've got a list of about 100 people I've got to see right away.

As you begin to see them, you begin to get a reputation: "I was asked to come in here by these churches, in fact they gave me this kind of money in my name at so-and-so bank to come in here and build an organization. It's a community organization where people can participate in the life of the community, and whatever's going on they deal with. These are some of the things I've heard about. I've heard about the real estate, I've heard about the schools." And the reaction is what you're looking for. I remember the real estate guy. He had laid out in the back room a plan that he thought needed to be done for the neighborhood.

He said, "What do you think?"

I said, "I like this." I said, "Every month I meet with the clergy. Would you bring this over and show it to them?"

"You're crazy."

"No, come on. You should be proud that you're doing this."

He said, "Well, I belong to so-and-so church."

I said, "Your pastor's part of it."

"Oh, I didn't know that."

So he came to the meeting. We became good friends. He was a realtor. He told me to go see someone, so that's how the chain began, see.

"Who do you think I ought to see? Who's important?"

"Oh you've got to go see — very important person."

"Can I use your name?"

"Oh, sure."

It becomes a web. People begin to call you up. I never have an office. I purposely never had an office in the early days. I had an answering service .... This wonderful woman, I've never met her to this day, my answering service, used to call me at home. "Tom, this is Mildred. I think you'd better follow up on this call." She became a friend. I've never met her. I swear to God, it was one of the greatest ideas I ever had. I never knew there was such a thing as an answering service. A human being, not those machines. She said, "I'm fascinated with your work."

I said, "I love these conversations."

It was great. And after many months, however long it was, they said to me, "You ought to have a place. We can find one." That's how we got our office.

PK: You didn't do that until you really moved —

TG: What do I need an office for? I said, "I work out of the back of my car. I've got a card file. What do I need a mimeograph for? You've got the mimeograph. I don't need it."

And you go around and interview. What you're studying is the power structure. And it's amazing, people in power, how they refer you to their friends. Which began to create the web. Who knows who. What they're saying is, "You've got to prove that I'm important."

And it's always a biggie: "Mr. So-and-so, Charlie your friend said I should come over and see you."

"What's Charlie up to now?"

"Well, I'm trying to build an organization."

"Oh, you're the guy. I've heard about you. Oh, it's my turn."

You find friends in all of these places. You find assholes: "The commie — you're a commie."

Businessmen: "Tell me who you are."

"I used to be the vice president of Admiral Corporation."

"Oh, you're not clergy."

"No, I'm married and have seven kids."

"You know so-and-so?"

"Sure, he's a good friend of mine, call him up."

I'm doing the same thing. Credentials. "I'm not some young, crazy do-gooder." I used it all the time. A suit, tie, all that stuff. But I never carried a briefcase, I just refused. I see people doing that, "What the hell you got in there for chrissake?" A briefcase! . . .

After about three months, you've got enough information, let me tell you. You've got stuff like this. What do you do next?

"Father, I would like to meet with 10 of your people. Ten people that you think I should see." That's a test. Are they his friends? Is this his power structure, his gang in the church? Or just anybody? It's very interesting. It's not all the same way again.

"Tom, this person is a wonderful church-goer, but hates me. I'd like you to interview him."

It's interesting. There'd be another one that you could say, "Oh, he controls this group."

I used to sell, I used to be a salesman. You learn there's four different types of people. And you split their mind four different ways. I could be tough with this person, but not with this person. This I have to be gentle, pull him out. It's the same thing with organizing. You don't go in and say the same thing to everybody. You present the same idea different ways. Sometimes, it's strong, sometimes it's weak. Sometimes you ask questions. It just depends. So you learn that, and then very quickly — "How do we do it? How do we start?" Staff started to show up . . .

PK: You got your first leaders and your staff then? . . .

TG: What was the first issue? It was interesting. It was Cicero Avenue, that's right. Something about crime on Cicero Avenue. Cicero Avenue was dirty, something like that. The community of Cicero was across the expressway. I said, "We're going to dump all this dirt from Austin back on Cicero." Something like that. It was goofy. And there were blacks, whites. It was an exciting organization, a marvelous woman, Marcella Kane . . . .

*   *   *   *   *   *   *

I'm a nut on a lot of that sanitation stuff. The image. A lot of the young people don't see that. You can go to NCO [Northwest Community Organization] today. I built the whole reputation on cleaning that place. Oh, the stories I could tell you about the garbage and the brooms. We had 150 brooms. Each organization gave me a buck to buy a broom and put their name on it. Around the office were brooms on hooks. It became a symbol.

"What the hell are all the brooms here?"

"We don't tolerate dirt." . . .

I'm telling the truth. It got so busy, we've got pictures of these hundreds of people pushing brooms. They'd be down there picking up the stuff and so forth. One day, and I'm telling the truth, Chestnut Street, right near St. Boniface Church, we were meeting on a vacant lot. It was awful filthy. Friday night.

"What are we going to do, Mr. Gaudette?"

"Clean up." The best way to demonstrate something to politicians is to show them you don't need them. That's the greatest way to teach a politician. It drives them nuts. Because his power is, he thinks you need him. I said, "Did the sonofabitch ever do anything for you?"

"No."

"What do you need him for? But take the garbage, clean it up, and put it out in the middle of the street and put a sign on it. 'Property of the alderman.' Watch what happens."

So they got the brooms. I had the flu. Next morning, I'm watching TV, 10 o'clock in the morning, there's a camera. "Ladies and gentlemen, a neighborhood group on the northwest side cleaned up this street, put the garbage on the trailer." And the alderman's wife owned a tavern. I would never have thought of that. They took the garbage and dumped it in front of the tavern. You can see the policemen writing tickets and everything.

I said, "I was home. Honest to God, it wasn't my idea." So I went into the office Monday morning. "Tony — Father, what the hell is this stuff?"

"Well, we showed that sonofabitch."

"You sure did get his attention."

He showed me these tickets. For nuisance, $35. We had to go to court. I made every school get the kids to collect pennies, $35 worth of pennies, and put them in a jar. And we went into court, and when the person's name was called, the kid would go up and put the jar on the judge's table. Then the judge would sit there. "What in the hell is going on? Officer, step up here. What's going on here?"

"These people dumped garbage in front of Matt Bieszczat's wife's tavern."

He said, "Do you have any pictures of it? What the hell are you arresting these people for? You should be home with your kids."

"The kids are here."

"Oh my God, the kids. Father, what are you doing here? Officer, don't you have other things to do?"

That's how we ended it. . . .

He had 510 precinct captains. You should have seen it, that whole summer. He was all sweetness. It was an example, and I can't get this across to the young people. These are symbols. I don't expect people to sweep the damned streets for the rest of their lives. I think they ought to do it more than they're doing it. I sweep my streets. But I said, "This man in power, who probably controls millions of dollars, lets people live like this. That's bullshit. That vacant lot. Look at it. We shouldn't have a vacant lot. Get railroad ties and put swings up and grass and sod and make it alive. Why should people live like that? And that guy permits it." That's the point. I've got to show people that there's something they can do about their misery . . . .

But it was great. That's part of the whole mystery of what Saul was describing. Democracy. It's a step. Remember the pyramid? The next time they do this — "Now we'd like to do something about that building down the street there."

Next thing you know — "What are we going to do about schools?"
It started happening. I was there four years . . . .

*   *   *   *   *   *   *

And now today, it's all over the place. There's so many organizations.
I go to California, I go to Kansas City, I go to St. Louis, I go to Mobile,
New Orleans. I'll be in Philadelphia next week. Trenton. Detroit. I go to
Camden — that's a great city. I think they're in Alaska, Japan. Gale just
came back from the Orient. She sent me a card from Hong Kong. But
think about it! The people that worked with me. Shel [Trapp]. What a
beautiful organizer. Wild, crazy, marvelous human being. A clergyman.
Just a great man. God knows what they're doing. The people they're
touching. Give me a break. I can't even keep up with them.

PK: He's going downstate so much.

TG: Oh, they're all over. . . . You can't believe how far this thing goes.
Sister Mary Jordan, this gal I worked with down in New Orleans,
Louisiana. Great city. One of my favorite cities . . . . She went to
Oklahoma, six towns in Oklahoma.
   "This is Mary Jordan. I've got an idea. I'm working with the Arapahos
and the Cherokees."
   "Jordan, what are you talking about?"
   "I've got an idea. If I could bring the Hispanics and the Indians and the
blacks and the whites together, what do you think about that?"
   "Jordan, you're on drugs. What are you talking about?"
   She had a convention. And the Indian chief read the Bill of Rights. The
Mexican guy sang in Spanish the national anthem. And she had a choir of
Arapahos, Cherokees, blacks, Mexicans, whites . . . .

PK: And this was in the 1980s? She's doing it right now?

TG: Yes. She's back down in New Orleans, Louisiana. She's met with 80
churches. She'll do it. It's exciting. In fact, they've built a training program
with a group I worked with in California.

PK: Who do you work with in California?

TG: John Baumann. He's a priest. Oakland, San Jose, San Diego,
Anaheim, Fullerton. They're talking about Stockton . . . .

TG: When I left NCO, I was always so scared it was unique, and the
leadership I had there. I actually tried to talk them into moving with me to
Austin because I'll never find this leadership again. This is all there is. Just

these leaders. Within two months in Austin, I forgot them. I had a whole new group of leaders. I didn't do it. They were there. I didn't make them leaders. They were there. They were frustrated and they wanted to get things done. How I helped them was to provide the means, that's all. But they were there. They're everywhere. But there is no place for them to plug in, they're all by themselves. Or they've got their hands full. And that's what I try to do — go find them. Ask them questions. Get them angry. See how far you can push them . . . .

PK: It's all over the country.

TG: It just grows. I always said, "If you're good at it, I'll get you a place. I'll find some way to create a thing. I think that's what a lot of them are doing now. The thing expands. That's what makes it exciting. If we could only come together once, just once, and say this is the way it's going to be. No more homeless. No more drugs . . . . And these kids are going to get an education.

We've got experience now. Why the hell don't we use it and get something done? Now there are things happening. But this is the chance to climb the mountain.

Organizing in the 1990s

Excerpts from a
Roundtable Discussion

*'The most important thing is we have a world that will have
10 billion people in it, and if we don't organize that world,
it's going to blow up in our faces.'*

Patrick Barry

Photo by Lucia Woods

On September 22, 1989, the authors of the articles that make up most of this book got together in Chicago with representatives from *Illinois Issues,* Woods Charitable Fund, Inc., and other guests for an afternoon discussion. The main question was simple: What did you learn about community organizing from writing about it? The reason for asking was obvious. Nine articles had produced nine different views of community organizing in Illinois. We needed to compare notes, discover what these insights had in common and where and why they diverged. We needed, in short, to have a conversation. Our aim was to put the articles into some kind of relationship with one another and with such overriding Illinois (and global) concerns as race and ethnicity, politics, economics, media, money and values.

John Kretzmann, trustee of the Wieboldt Foundation and director of the Urban Studies Program for the Associated Colleges of the Midwest, served as moderator. Authors taking part in the discussion were Ben Joravsky, "Alinsky's Legacy"; Paul M. Green, "SON/SOC"; Barack Obama, "Why Organize?"; Thom Clark, "Tenants and Neighbors"; Patrick Barry, "Gale Cincotta and Heather Booth"; Cheryl Frank, "Organizing Downstate"; Bill Kemp, "South Suburban Islands of Poverty"; and Christopher Robert Reed, "Washington's Civic Legacy." Wilfredo Cruz, "UNO," was unable to attend.

Also participating were J. Michael Lennon, publisher of *Illinois Issues;* Sokoni Karanja, trustee of the Woods Charitable Fund, Inc. and executive director of Centers for New Horizons; Anne Hallett, director of the Wieboldt Foundation; Louis Delgado, assistant director of the special grants program at the John D. and Catherine T. MacArthur Foundation. Other guests from Woods were Lucia Woods Lindley, trustee and photographer, and program directors Ken Rolling and Daryl Woods. Also present was Peg Knoepfle, associate editor of *Illinois Issues.* Court reporter Wanda Monterrubio recorded the discussion. The first speaker was Ben Joravsky, whose January 1988 article introduced the series.

Joravsky: . . . . Aside from the colorful aspects of the personality of Saul Alinsky, my article lays out certain basic rules of organizing established by Alinsky. I wrote it to clearly give credit to the labor movement because much of what he devised are old labor strategies, and to a lesser degree basic ward-heeling strategies. You know, get-out-the-old-precinct kind of organizing strategies.

And the first one, of course, that pops to mind is personalizing the issue. Saul Alinsky believed that to go into a neighborhood and organize people around that sort of general notion that we should be good to each other won't get you anywhere. I think what he used to say is you can't just talk about bad buildings in general. You have to talk about this bad building and, particularly, that bad landlord, so that people have a character they can organize around and get all upset about or at least get their attention focused on. So personalizing the issue is very important.

He also believed in what he called "native leadership." It wasn't good enough, Alinsky said, for somebody to come into a community from the outside and be the chief organizer. That person's job was to identify people who were themselves natural leaders, the ones that people on the block already looked to for leadership. What organizing should do is give that person a vehicle to really express his or her leadership capabilities.

The third thing that he is most known for are his tactics, tactics of confrontation. That's what most people talk about when they talk about Saul Alinsky. They think of all the various protests, and, you know, in his books he laid out some goofy schemes . . . . I think at the end he was sort of playing to the character, playing to the audience. But, anyway, he said don't be shy, don't be afraid of marches, protests, sit-ins. If the problem is with the landlord, and the landlord lives outside of the community in the suburbs, pack everybody into a bus and take them down to the landlord's house and picket.

So in a very general sense, this is Saul Alinsky's contribution to community organizing, but beyond that, there was Saul Alinksy, the man. And when we start talking about the changes or the problems with the Saul Alinsky model, it comes because Saul Alinsky was such a colorful character and powerful personality that he seemed to overshadow most of the groups he was organizing, particularly toward the end of his life — he died of a heart attack in 1972.

I see that happening a lot in Chicago. It's just a natural phenomenon. You can't help it. You could have somebody who is "native leadership" and is picked out by these organizers, paid organizers, Alinsky types who come in, and over time maybe the community organization represents just that one person, or maybe the original Alinsky guy who came in to organize it. But just as Saul Alinsky seemed to overshadow the entire community organizing philosophy that he devised, many of his disciples began to overshadow their organizations. That's been a problem in many groups in Chicago. The Woodlawn Organization (TWO) springs to mind and to a lesser degree the United Neighborhood Organization (UNO). There are so many squabbles that it's hard to know who's in, who's out.

And then, finally, what I got out of the article was that perhaps the greatest drawback to community organizing as devised by Saul Alinsky is one that he himself recognized and wrote about, and that is: If you organize at the local level, all too often you cut yourself off from the larger issues that control your life. It can be kind of meaningless at a point to just organize around stop signs, as a classic example, or police beat patrols or a new high school even. The idea was that you start small, you take on causes that you know will result in victories, that will give people confidence so they can move on to challenge the larger powers that be and take control of their life and build some coalitions.

All too often so much energy is expended on some of these smaller battles that it's hard to get people mobilized to the bigger ones. And once you do get people into coalitions, you find out there is so much rivalry and bitterness between them as they fight for their grants and to get their names in the paper, that you can't develop those larger coalitions. So these are some of the problems that Alinsky was addressing at the end of his life, and these are some of the problems that still exist today.

Kretzmann: Okay. Here are some basic tenets and some basic questions . . . .

Joravsky: The most important problem, I think, is the latter one. I mean, the issue of personalities overwhelming organizations is going to happen anyway. And that gets to be gossip, which is fun to talk about. But I note that some of the articles dealt with community organizing issues — Paul's article on SON/SOC springs to mind. To me it gets at that basic issue: How do you move out beyond the confines of your neighborhood where you may have done a very successful job and form a larger coalition that can challenge more powerful forces? I haven't seen a great working model of that in Chicago . . . .

In terms of getting a national voice on all these different community groups, I haven't seen that happen. Alinsky advocated that in his first book published in 1946. He had this model. He would say, okay, you start on a local level. And then you realize that the people in the neighborhood down the street have the same concerns you do. Then you go to this other city, and they have the same concerns you do, and you come together. You know, he made it sound so easy, and, of course, it wasn't.

Who wrote the article on Heather Booth's group [Midwest Academy and Citizen Action]?

Barry: I did.

Joravsky: That's what she's trying to do [build national coalitions]: get names into a computer and get a mailing list set up. So that on a particular issue you have your base you can go to. You can generate a lot of support, financially. And I think she may have plateaued. She may have reached a certain number. It's a struggle. There is no easy answer to it.

Clark: And, of course, the irony is that here in Chicago although Midwest Academy is recognized around the country as a vital force in Citizen Action — it is real important in Massachusetts and in other places

— you won't find many [Chicago] community groups who want to sit around the table with people like that —

Joravsky: Right.

Clark: Because tactics and personalities and whatnot just don't work. Now, IPAC [Illinois Public Action Council], in fact, has done door-to-door canvassing to increase its grass-roots membership. But it's not the same kind of grass-roots membership. It really doesn't speak to the issue of neighborhood development that groups in Chicago are struggling with. So the irony is that this national example of moving from organizing to political power is not something that local groups in Chicago look up to as an example of how they want to operate at all.

Joravsky: You're right. There are two different goals mentioned. One, developing grass-roots leadership, as you said, and the other one is getting a national coalition. Those are two different goals. And often they seem to be at each other's throats —

Green: The problem with national goals in this city is that the city of Chicago is inward, not outward . . . .

Kretzmann: . . . . There are other ways in which the Alinsky vision, at least as articulated in the book, is not practiced. What Alinsky talked a lot about and was never able to do, as you point out, was good interracial organizing. One of the major and most controversial organizations in Chicago, Paul, is the one you wrote about. SON/SOC [Save our Neighborhoods, Save our City] is clearly a group that sees itself directly in the Alinsky tradition and defines that in a certain way. Do you want to talk about what you found?

Green: . . . . Two things struck me at the beginning. First, the two organizers, Mike Smith and Bob Gannett, who are the paid organizers for SON/SOC, are really Alinsky disciples. They are modeling from him. Of course, they have an advantage in a sense because the kinds of people they are working with are the kinds of people Alinsky was working with. So it isn't breaking new racial or ethnic barriers. They have blue-collar, white, working-class people. The other thing was that Smith, whom I quoted in the article, said that everybody has a right to obtain power. That's Alinskyesque right there. The issue in the article was simply: Can that be true in a city as racially polarized as Chicago when the group that wants to obtain power is all-white basically? . . .

So what I tried to play with was the history of these people who fought City Hall when it wasn't in vogue to fight City Hall, who were standing up to then Mayor Richard J. Daley and winning, who were basically individuals with no political goals, no political aspirations. Hardly anybody in that organization has ever run for political office . . . . What I find to be so interesting is that for many of them, it was no big deal having the mayor of Chicago against them, whether it happened to be a black mayor or a white mayor — they have always been against them. Then you come into the culture of basically the southwest side of Chicago, which feels that it has a giant chip on its shoulder that it's been carrying around for decades, from the Alinsky period and before. Once again times change, but their relationship to power doesn't change.

Well, after dealing with that — and let me tell you it was an awful lot for me to look at objectively since my family background is directly in these neighborhoods — there was the issue of what they wanted. At the time home equity was the No. 1 issue they were talking about, and I wrote about it. [Guaranteed home equity protects the value of houses in changing neighborhoods, usually neighborhoods undergoing racial change. It does this by paying participating owners the difference between the market value of their homes and the selling price. A state law enabling home equity commissions to be established in Chicago precincts by referendum was passed in 1988. Proponents said it was a necessary protection against panic peddling. Opponents said it was racist.] And now, as you know, home equity passed the legislature in Springfield, but it never passed the City Council, or if it did, it was vetoed. But home equity to them was nonracial; it was merely protecting their property without question . . . .

And then it came to pure Alinsky economics. The people who are rich, the people who can be segregated from the problem because they live in high-rises with private security or live in all-white suburbs or suburbs with a sprinkling of minorities who are all very rich, are telling the poor people to do something that they are not willing to do themselves. Needless to say, I had a difficult time saying, "Let's look at this objectively." I agreed with them. I agreed with them completely.

So what I saw were individuals who don't want to leave their neighborhoods, many of whom can't afford to leave. Many are elderly women. The No. 1 occupation is widow. All they have is their home, and all they want to do is live the rest of their lives in their own community. They are afraid of crime. They are afraid of change, and yet their neighborhoods are being integrated. And it was just a very difficult thing.

To sum it up, if there wasn't a racial factor this would have been a wonderful thing to write. Here are a bunch of blue-collar people, working-class people, working to help their neighborhood. A lot of this education reform was taken from their proposal that they worked out with a group called CURE [Chicagoans United to Reform Education]. I mean, they were on top of that issue, but they were looking at their community and trying, as they saw it, to find a way to protect and preserve . . . .

Basically, to update: Integration is taking place west of Western Avenue on the southwest side of Chicago. I am afraid there is going to be resegregation. Home equity — I don't know if it's working yet, if anyone can apply for it yet. It's an ongoing problem, and the real dilemma is that the wrong people in our socioeconomic strata are being asked to do something that people in the higher income levels don't want to do.

Reed: It's interesting. I don't want to disagree with anything you've said. I am not a political scientist, but it's interesting as to what might have happened had there not been an election as early as '87. That is, Mayor Harold Washington had gone on record after the second year of his administration as being willing to listen to people on the southwest side, and he appeared to be in support of their efforts. But then along came the election of 1987, and all of these people who had been recalcitrant in 1983, had not really been converted by 1987. There was a need, as you mentioned in your book on bashing Chicago traditions, a need to place this politically — this is on Washington's part. Therefore, he had to back into a defensive position. That was to attach himself to the emotional issue that whites don't want blacks.

But, say, Washington had been serving a six-year term and the election would have been in 1989. It's quite possible that he would have remained in support of home equity at the local level and would not have rejected it, as Mayor Eugene Sawyer did, and might have supported it at the state level. But I think you're right, the political issue did come in.

A comment, though, about the resegregation and the inability of a resegregated neighborhood to increase property values. Do you remember about 15 or 20 years ago the Chicago Urban League used to make it its business to let people know what happened in Park Manor and Chatham? In those areas there was an increase in property values. The key here is not that resegregation automatically brings a depreciation. It's if there is resegregation with the wrong socioeconomic group in a neighborhood, then you will have a depreciation of property values. But for years the Park Manor and Chatham examples were flaunted, and it made sense back in the '60s and '70s. It makes sense in 1989. That's why the *Sun-Times* and other publications wrote about it. However, the reality — and I agree with you here — has not been addressed.

Let me just expand on what you're saying. If you try to get newcomers, especially after the first wave, who are not of the same socioeconomic inclinations as the oldtimers who are there or even the first wave of newcomers, if you try to get them interested in protecting what has been, then you're going to have a problem. And, in fact, the proof is that if the second, third, whatever waves of newcomers with these different values, don't keep up property, they will, in fact, fall into a self-fulfilling prophecy. You know, the cry that if we open our doors to you, our neighborhood will go down.

Joravsky: I would like to pick up on something that Paul said because we have a slight disagreement here, but that's all right. I have followed the history of those groups, and what Paul says is absolutely true. In a lot of ways they got a bad rap before 1983. Before '83 they were at the forefront of just about every significant movement in Chicago. Getting the police department to give out things like crime stats for precincts — they were on the forefront of that. They fought Mayor Jane Byrne tooth and nail on that one. They were also way ahead on linked development, which was their major issue until home equity came around. Linked development — which

I happen not to agree with them on — would tax downtown development and use the money to fund development in the neighborhoods. Those are progressive issues, nonracial.

And I note this, because I was in the room with them writing articles about them. They were suddenly given one of the great organizing opportunities of all time. You talk about personalizing the issues — you had the issue personalized in the person of Mayor Harold Washington, a man who about 92 to 93 percent of their constituents, of people in their areas, had voted against, a man who inspired all sorts of fears, be they rational or not. And there was tremendous hostility. This is right after the council wars where Eddie Vrdolyak and Eddie Burke were standing up and saying, "I'll champion your rights." There was tremendous racial hostility.

And these groups, they had a choice. They could either take the Alinsky method, which is to personalize the enemy and use him to your best advantage, or they could somehow or other back off and let this political fighting occur on its own without participation. They were very political. From their standpoint, they made the right choice. They organized the white ethnic agenda. They held out a candle. When he drove up, they held out the candle of understanding. And they asked him to stop the car and light the candle, and he didn't. In fact, they said he blew the candle out. And then they sent out fundraising letters that used language like the following: Operation PUSH and the Urban League have their constituents, now you need yours. The point is you can say those are conventional Alinsky tactics. They were just playing it out. Here was a guy they knew they could rally support on.

The other point is do you have some kind of fundamental obligation to somehow or other temper your appeal? [Chicago organizer] Shel Trapp told me this a long time ago: "I could go into Cicero right now, and I could organize against the blacks. And I could be the greatest organizer in the world. But is that morally correct? Shouldn't I go into Cicero and use tactics, and say, 'Look we all are low-income people who live in this big universe together?'" So that's a sort of dilemma that organizers struggle with. I know these people. I don't think they struggled. They saw an opportunity and they took it.

Green: I don't know what the time frame is, but it was one year later when Harold Washington was appearing at the annual [banquet] and praising them and praising Alvin Robinson, the black realtor, and [20th Ward Ald.] Cliff Kelley, who was instrumental in all of this. There was a change. I mean, they were willing. I am sure they were angry. They were scared, to use a good word. They were scared to death. And, yes, they needed something to rally the people around. They thought the people were just willing to give up, and they didn't want to give up their homes. But they, more than any other white ethnic group in Chicago, reached out to Harold Washington, who then reached back to them.

I agree with what you say. If there wasn't a political side of this coming down so hard and the emotional side of it colliding, I think there could have been an agreement. I don't know the inside story. I interviewed Harold Washington twice and he wouldn't talk about it . . . . The bottom line is that Washington was willing to give them that opportunity because he was convinced, I believe — and this is my interpretation of events, he never told me this — but I believe that he was convinced there was a possibility for a breakthrough with these people because they weren't political. They weren't Eddie Burke's guys or Ed Vrdolyak's guys. They had fought those guys. These were the people who prevented the Crosstown Expressway. He knew about that and that they were very much in vogue with a lot of issues he supported.

Barry: Two fundamental organizing jobs that I think SON/SOC has fallen down on and the groups before them have fallen down on. And, that is, they haven't been willing to stay in their neighborhoods on the south side. They moved once. They moved again. They moved a third time. If they would organize and say, "We are going to stay" — I know it would have been difficult, but Hyde Park did it, Rogers Park is doing it, Oak Park did it.

Green: Let's not put Hyde Park in the same category.

Barry: It isn't, but it is. The other thing is they didn't organize across racial lines. There are not very many interracial meetings out there . . . .

Green: Let me just respond in one sentence and probably get some people around this table upset. There is more meaningful integration taking place in Marquette Park today than is taking place in Hyde Park.

Barry: And what community is working on it? Southwest Community Congress, not Southwest Parish [and Neighborhood Federation, which joined with Northwest Neighborhood Federation to form SON/SOC].

Green: But the bottom line is that the community itself is going into more meaningful integration. As a long-time Hyde Park resident and somebody who studied that fairly extensively, the liberal tradition of Hyde Park needs a new interpretation. It's a phony integration. Real integration between people of low-income groups is taking place outside of Hyde Park. Hyde Park has simply burned neighborhoods all around them.

Clark: I agree with you. As someone who lives in an economically and racially diverse community, Uptown, as a neighbor of [SON/SOC organizer] Bob Gannett, I know something about what we are talking about. It seems to me that there is a critical issue to examine. Why after these inroads were made, why was the switch made? We can say there were politics, but it occurs to me that there was some kind of fundamental error in the home equity organizing effort, particularly in Marlene Carter's ward, because there were supposed to be black organizers in the 15th Ward, which was the ward of demarcation at that point if it's not now. And I know because I was writing at *The Neighborhood Works.* I was very turned on about their picking up on linked development, and I could understand the home equity issue, having grown up in Oak Park, having lots of friends in Austin.

There was an opportunity, and there was funding behind an effort to do interracial organizing. And it didn't work. I am not blaming it on SON/SOC and I am not blaming Marlene Carter and that political organization per se, but it seems to me that is the crux of where the thing fell apart, where the combination that Kelley and others had put together fell apart. I don't know all the p's and q's about it, but it seems clear that in terms of an update — the end of your story, obviously, is written after Harold has died and Eugene Sawyer is in and before Richie [Mayor Richard M. Daley] comes in — I think the situation is in a very different context now . . . .

Green: . . . . If there was a black mayor now, this would still be an ongoing story. Now, I think things might be more interesting in relationship to one of their own. And I don't know what the relationship is, to be honest with you. But the process is still going on, and integration is taking place across lines that for a kid who grew up on the southwest side of Chicago, I thought I would never see . . . .

Reed: In defense of the Hyde Park community, in defense of community organizing 30 years ago — I am doing research in archives now, and what I determined was that in Hyde Park, the NAACP in the 1950s was totally integrated not only in terms of race, but also in terms of ideology — the left and traditional and some working-class people with a lot of middle-class people. And that particular unit was committed — at the time the University of Chicago was going to implement its urban renewal plan — to keeping blacks from being forced back into the black ghetto. That is interesting. This was an attitude 30 years ago, which I didn't expect to find . . . .

Kretzmann: Another kind of question is the set of questions, Barack, that you addressed in "Why organize?" — particularly in low-income black communities, which have changed drastically over the last decade.

Obama: . . . . Part of the main function of my article, and the main function of this book and this conversation is to try to place organizing in a larger context, to figure out what kind of animal it is. I remember talking to Peter Martinez [a Chicago organizer, trained by Alinsky] awhile back. And he said something that I think to some extent I share a view with. He said, "I care about organizing. I don't care about community organizing." And I think what he meant by that is that organizing has a long tradition in this country. It didn't start with Alinsky. It didn't stop with Alinsky. What it has to do with is: How do you include the excluded in this country? And its history started with the founding fathers. It goes on to the abolitionists. It includes people who organize machine politics in Chicago, people who organize the black church in the South. How do you get people who are on the outside of the mainstream into the mainstream? And also, how do you get that mainstream to change through that process, to get rich and examine itself and remake itself? That's the important question. And I think what Saul Alinsky came up with was one cut on that.

The thing that came out in a lot of these articles is that the bedrock principle gets lost a lot of times — what the purpose of this process is. And so I want to spin out a couple of ideas. One theme that I heard, particularly when we discussed the SON/SOC article is — and I am not sure this was made explicit — it seems to me there were two roles that an organizer was supposed to play or organizations were supposed to play. One was very straightforward, political: getting power, getting the stop sign, making things work.

The other theme — and this gets lost, and a lot of it has to do with the fault of the organizers, a lot of it has to do with the pressures of outside forces — is the educative function of organizing. The process whereby people in communities, like the community SON/SOC was organizing or the community where I was organizing, start to get bigger horizons, start to understand how they connect up with other people, how their power is involved with the power of other people. It seems to me that that strain gets lost . . . . At some point you have to link up winning that stop sign or getting that home equity with the larger trends, larger movements in the city or the country. I think we are not very good at that.

The second thing is that I am not sure we talk enough in organizing about — and this is connected to the educative function — sort of the culture: We tend to think of organizing as a mechanical, instrumental thing. I think Alinsky to some extent may not have emphasized this, but I think the unions that Alinsky saw — I think John L. Lewis understood that he was building a culture. When you look at what's happened to union organizing, one of the losses has been that sense of building a culture, of building up stories and getting people to reflect on what their lives mean and how people in the neighborhood can be heroes, and how they are part of a larger force. That got shoved to the side. I think that is a detriment to organizing.

Just a couple other strands, and I will open it up. The relationship between organizing and politics. It's interesting the example that you raised with SON/SOC and Washington and how the political situations sort of sabotaged a possible rapprochement between those two groups. Part of it may have to do with the fact that we don't understand what the relationship between organizing and politics should be . . . . I would like to think that ideally you would focus on the local but educate for the broader arena, and that you are creating a base for electoral politics or national issues.

I am not sure those things [politics and leadership development] are inevitably, mutually exclusive. I don't think they have to be. I think it has to do in part with a tradition of suspicion of politics. But the problem we face now in terms of organizing is that politics is a major arena of power. That's where your major dialogue, discussion, is taking place. To marginalize yourself from that process is a damaging thing, and one that needs to be rethought.

Two other things. One would be the whole issue of the relationship between organizing and the media. Again, that was something that I was trying to raise in my article. Recently, a black woman [Ruby Oliver] made a movie *[Leola]* about basically her life in her neighborhood . . . . And I went to see that. What was interesting was that she had gotten folks from the neighborhood to star in the film. They were all in the audience, and they were all watching themselves. They were playing out the problems with teenage pregnancy . . . . What was happening was that through filmmaking, the community was getting a better understanding of itself and what it was doing.

That's organizing, and I think organizations don't think about that. I mean, I think the moral majority thinks about it. I think the culture of the right wing right now thinks about it. Ronald Reagan thought about it. We don't understand it. We don't think about rethinking ourselves, projecting ourselves, about how we are getting to understand ourselves.

It's particularly important in poor black communities where we have to figure out some medium to reach black youth. They are not necessarily going to town hall meetings, and they are not going to pick up *Reveille for Radicals*. They are going to see the Spike Lee film, or they are going to listen to the rap group. So the question of what role organizing might have in that process needs to be examined. We keep losing track of that. That connects with the political. There are some broader strands there.

The only other thing that I want to emphasize, that I think is key: Organizing is long-term. Organizing right now doesn't have a long-term vision, it seems to me. It has a very specific particularized vision. Alinsky-style organizing, to some extent, when he started getting into the long term, became idealized. All that particularity got lost in the vague idealistic democracy.

I noticed Gale Cincotta was quoted as saying, "I am not trying to build some grand utopian organization. I would just like to win it." That's problematic. I remember a story another organizer told me about how he had gone to an IAF [Industrial Areas Foundation] training session. And IAF always emphasized how movements are rotten with charismatic leaders, etc. I remember this friend of mine turned to me and said, "That's nonsense. We want a movement. I would love to have Martin Luther King here right now."

The point is not that movements are superior to [community] organizing — a lot was lost during the civil rights movement because there was not enough effective organizing consolidating those gains. But that long-term vision needs to be developed. And organizing can contribute to that even as it's making local changes, even as it's training very particularized native leadership, even as it's building small mediating institutions. It's still trying to develop and project and elaborate on a long-term vision, going back to what I said earlier, on including people who were excluded . . . .

Lennon: I am glad you brought up the relationship between organizing and the media. It made me think of a comment that you made earlier, Ben, about how when we look back at Saul Alinsky, we tend to see confrontational tactics when he had in mind things a lot more sophisticated than that. One of the reasons, I think, is the media. Media is interested in confrontation, and so it's going to emphasize those things in organizing that are clashes. And that's all it's going to look at.

The culture that you talk about, that's another fine point you made, too. What kind of culture are you trying to build? Is that the only culture you want? One that reinforces the notion of confrontation? Is that all there is to it? Well, that is not a culture. A culture ought to be a dialectic. It should be more than just a clash. There should be a higher synthesis coming out of it . . . .

Obama: . . . . I like what you said about the fact that theoretically the idea was that confrontation was supposed to lead to reconciliation, and that gets lost. We don't focus on that. What I am wondering with the example of SON/SOC was: Where were the churches in this process, and was there an examination? Was there any kind of thinking going on about how does this relate back to what we preach and what we believe and what our faith is?

That kind of stuff gets lost. When I speak about media and culture, these are the things I am talking about . . . . Just one other point that you brought up, one of the things that organizing needs to think about: How do you educate people enough so that they can be forcing their politicians to articulate their broader views and wider horizons?

Kretzmann: Accountability, holding them accountable.

Obama: Holding them accountable, not just in a mechanistic way, holding them accountable in the sense that people expect politicians to express some long-term interests of theirs and not just appeal to the lowest common denominator. One of the things I see organizing being able to do without getting directly involved in electoral politics is plowing some soil so that when elections do come around and politicians come in with race baiting or demagoguery, enough work has been laid there so that — not that [demagoguery] is going to be ineffective, but that it will be less effective — there will be some counter voices to it.

Kretzmann: It seems to me that we have three clusters of conversations to have over the next hour or so. I am thinking about pairs of pieces: Patrick Barry's and Thom Clark's, as the Chicago pieces out of traditional Alinsky roots — or at least a variance on those roots. Thom wrote about two venerable local institutions: Organization of the NorthEast (ONE) and Northwest Community Organization (NCO), and Patrick focused on two of the fascinatingly charismatic folks who lead large coalitions, Heather Booth and Gale Cincotta — the Citizen Action network and the National People's Action group.

Clark: I felt kind of lucky because not only was I covering two self-described Alinsky-style organizations, but I was covering two specific, relatively short-term and successful organizing campaigns. You can't do that very often in this business.

In the case of NCO, I was covering a reactive campaign. It was a reactive campaign to discovering PCBs in the neighborhood that Commonwealth Edison had kept quiet. Basically NCO was able to gain some technical expertise from groups outside of its neighborhood. It also brought in some new leaders, along with old leaders, who were able to get the community upset about environmental pollution and to really bang up ComEd pretty good to the point of getting some fairly quick response.

In the case of ONE, the major issue was housing and, in particular, tenants in HUD [U.S. Department of Housing and Urban Development] high-rises. Again, a reactive campaign. A building was having its mortgage prepaid. Tenants got eviction notices. There was, coincidentally, at the same time federal legislation placing a moratorium on such prepayments. So ONE was able to do a legal rights campaign by raising that issue and banging it up on HUD, and saying, "You guys weren't supposed to do this. . . ."

In the case of ONE . . . . the campaign continues. In fact, last night I was at a meeting [that illustrated] the dynamic I talked about at the end of my story: the fact that the campaign was largely organized by paid staff of various groups in Uptown and Edgewater as opposed to [local] leaders. Last night we had a meeting with about 18 or 20 people from HUD high-rises. There are about 10 groups, 2,500 families, in the next year to five years who face wholesale eviction as a result of this mortgage-prepayment issue. There is now a community-wide campaign being launched, I think. We have to wait and see. There is clearly an effort to make it a tenant-led group rather than a staff-led group. Nonetheless, only 18 people were there. Six of us, were, I think, more in the paid-staff category.

I guess what I learned out of this thing is that there are still a lot of people talking about leadership development and concerned when it doesn't happen, concerned about it in a neighborhood like Uptown where you have sophisticated groups and fairly well-funded staff working with people who are engaged in a political and economic environment that is really stacked against them. In fact, many of the people who are victimized by this environment are not looking at Uptown as necessarily their home neighborhood from now on, but are looking to get out of that neighborhood. As a result . . . . the issues remain very much the same, but the leaders move on. Move up and on. Or one might say in the last three or four years — move down and on because we are being forced out.

I think it will be interesting to see if this latest effort to form a new coalition of HUD high-rise tenants succeeds because I think the new staff director at ONE [former UNO organizer and current Citizen Utility Board president] Josh Hoyt recognizes that the only way such a campaign can succeed is by finding allies: churches and other social service and cultural agencies as well as business people. It is only with those sorts of alliances in a diverse community like Uptown that low-income tenants will be able to overcome what they're up against: HUD, private owners who don't manage their buildings very well, and a whole bunch of other things that are really beyond their ability to control. The HUD scandal in Washington, for example, or the freezing of programs that normally help the people in these buildings . . . .

One of the leading development groups in that neighborhood is the Voice of the People in Uptown. I think it's significant that Voice of the People and ONE are really for the first time in many years trying to work together on the HUD issue. Whereas, in the past for reasons of funding, competition, philosophical differences as well as tactical, that has not been an easy thing for them to do.

Green: May I jump in? Listening to what you say raises a very important question in my mind because you live in Uptown, and in Uptown the boundaries keep changing, but basically it's an area if it's not hot, it's certainly lukewarm.

Clark: It's hot. My taxes have doubled.

Green: Well, that's a given. It's becoming desirable again . . . . Here you have people in a hot neighborhood who are trying to hold on and, really, race is not an issue there. The only color that is coming in that is new is the color green. And yet they have many of the same problems that our pals on the southwest and the northwest side have in the neighborhoods that aren't hot. They are in the same position of dealing with economic forces . . . .

Clark: Well, I think this is the reason why Uptown continues to be a story. As a resident and an advocate on a variety of fronts over the years, I have seen three cycles of speculation . . . . The last two resulted in more vacant lots and empty buildings. I'm not sure that's what is going to happen this time, but I'm also not sure there is going to be the wholesale change that people are talking about. We indeed have more yuppies, buppies and guppies [young urban professionals, black urban professionals, gay urban professionals] . . . . But we also have a lot of Russian Jews, Ethiopians, Southeast Asians. The Vietnamese are up and coming — moving out to Skokie; the Cambodians aren't. There is a social service network that is strong if not vibrant. It is seen by the developers coming in as an obstruction. It is, of course, seen by those of us who live there as part of our saving grace, part of the reason why we don't think we are going to be wiped out.

Obama: I think a question that arises when you're dealing with large economic forces like this is to what extent are these organizations prepared to form some sort of pro-active strength? . . . So with the example of NCO or ONE: Are people sitting down and putting together plans for what those communities should do? Are there discussions with developers? Are they getting their own developers to think about what development means for those communities? Those questions are important whether you're talking about Grand Boulevard or a whole range of other communities.

Clark: In fact, ONE sponsored a community summit in June where a different sort of grouping than I had seen in many years was brought together to try and form such a vision. It was from the organizer's point of view not successful because no action agenda came out of it. It was from my vantage point an incredibly diverse grouping of people representing agencies and churches and whatnot, who came together to try to say, "Hey, the developers have their vision for what they want our neighborhood to be. We have our own. We need to start articulating." So, yes, there has been that effort. I am not sure how effective it has been.

Kretzmann: Thom, one of the issues that you raised was the question of leadership development. Obviously, one of the ways this has been done in Chicago is by developing networks and national efforts in leadership training. These outfits, as well as lots of other ones we have heard reported on, have related to both Heather Booth's and Gale Cincotta's work. Let's look broader for a little bit.

Barry: In fact, I think what we have been talking about is the evolution of organizing. Alinsky is fine, but that was a long time ago. There are a lot of new things. What Gale Cincotta and Heather Booth are doing is using force of personality, like Alinsky did, and also using technology to develop an organization, almost like business management, to build their machines and, I think, pave the way for development.

Certainly Gale Cincotta is paving the way for development on a large scale by these groups that Alinsky was helping a long time ago. Heather Booth and Gale Cincotta work people over. That's one of their key strengths, but that is a strength of every organizer: to get somebody to do something. More than that, they both use technology very well. Heather Booth built, I think, mostly from her own vision of a national organization. She built the phone banks. She built the network between states. She brought in the senior citizens, the unions, and built a machine like a politician. I don't know that organizers have done before what she did on such a broad scale. So I think her central accomplishment to date is that she has an almost-national organization up and running.

A lot of people say it's not really national. No, it's not really national, but it's one of the best things going in terms of a broad-based grass-roots organization. Now, she just happens to move to Washington, D.C. She was working here; she is now working there. That's the place for her to be if she leads a national organization. I expect we will see some more of her in the next couple of years, and certainly in the next presidential election, in the next election in Congress.

Gale Cincotta did it differently. She went after the law. She used the law to back banks into a corner and say: "Hey, the law says this. You are doing that. If you don't start complying, we are going to make trouble for you." And it worked. Cincotta does a lot more confrontation, a lot more of the barging into people's offices to get the media play, but she backs that up with $1.6 billion in lending out of the banks that she has gotten. It's not just the media play. It's media play to get attention for what is practically a revolutionary approach for people in the United States: telling the banks what to do. That is big.

So I think the significance of that is that organizing has reached a level of maturity where we have national movements going on. And we have leaders, like Barack was saying, people with vision who can work up a crowd and get them thinking about where we should be 20 years from now, about the transformation of society. And that's what I call vision.

Green: That's from a rusty essay at the University of Chicago.

Barry: So that's the base. What I think it means is that organizing is just getting going, and that it will ultimately become a basis of our society. That's what democracy is. It's built on community organizations and state organizations and regional organizations and groups like CANDO [Chicago Association of Neighborhood Development Organizations) and groups like CWED [Community Workshop on Economic Development] that bring people together from all over the city.

Kretzmann: There is an argument here for these groups representing — if I hear you right — the rebirth of civic life at a national level, built on local associations.

Barry: However, they still have a serious flaw. I get the calls from IPAC [Illinois Public Action Council], and they want my money. I don't know if they are doing that much for me, but they are doing something. They at least have the framework up.

Kretzmann: People want to follow up a little bit on the differences between the ways Booth and Cincotta go after these questions. Cincotta not only uses the law, she also makes it sometimes. [Cincotta helped write and pass the 1976 federal Community Reinvestment Act, requiring banks that are being bought or sold to prove they lend money in the communities in their service area.]

Clark: She made the law. She got this money, but the people who have to use it, by and large, don't find it to be affordable money for the people that she allegedly raised the money for.

Green: Say that again?

Clark: The money that was set up in the Neighborhood Lending Program is only about half used. The reason it's only half used is that it's market-rate financing. Yes, it's been allocated because of her organizing to neighborhoods that were credit poor, redlined, if you will. But they are low, moderate-income neighborhoods, and market-rate financing isn't going to be affordable for most of those people. So there's a problem as you leave your roots and move on to regional and national movements of losing sight of the needs of the people that you're supposedly working for.

Karanja: One of the problems is that Reagan cut off the funds.

Clark: Yes.

Karanja: So that the bridge money is not there.

Clark: And I am not belittling what Gale and others have produced, but there was a very immediate reaction when the issue of neighborhood lending programs was raised because that was largely done outside the neighborhood housing development movement [nonprofit organizations that develop low- and middle-income housing]. It was done more as an organizing campaign. As a result, those of us who were in the neighborhood housing development movement found the downtown banks saying, "We set up these great new neighborhood lending programs." But it wasn't affordable money even with — at that point there were still city and federal write-downs. That is not to denigrate the effort, but it's to recognize that this type of personality-style organizing can create big numbers of accomplishments that may not be solving the problem the campaign was originally set up to deal with.

Karanja: A step in the process.

Clark: A step in the process, right.

Hallett: And just to add on to that, as I understand, the other limitation was the fact that once you're global, you're not tending the neighborhood base, and that [reduces] the number of local groups and their capacity to use the money even if it were affordable.

Delgado: Wasn't either the housing or the economic development money used up first? I have been led to believe that a certain part of that money was more accessible.

Clark: Well, some of the banks actually priced their money better and it got used up very quickly in the multi-family portfolio. First National Bank would tell you six years ago that when they did this neighborhood lending thing that Gale had challenged them on, they set up a charity program. First National made it a part, last year, of its retail banking program. It's been making them money. What a lot of us were saying over the years — there is a market here that you have been ignoring — has proved to be true.

The distinction I was trying to make is that there is a part of the market, even with these neighborhood lending programs, that is not being served without the capacity of groups to carry it out or the federal bucks to make up the bridge financing.

Green: I have a question here . . . . Do they really view themselves as changing society?

Barry: I think Gale Cincotta says, no, she doesn't, [though] she certainly has done enough daydreaming to build some national muscle. Heather Booth feels, the way she puts it, if you help people win manageable goals, get them involved to such a point that their commitment gets deeper, they stay in. They realize, "I can change society. I have power." She says that, yes, we are going to have a different type of civic person, that if everybody is hooked in, then you have a better society.

I think Gale Cincotta's National People's Action is a very low-funded group that does indeed nurture grass-roots actions and strength. Heather Booth has built a machine, a technological triumph that, in fact, is probably losing touch. The trick will be in the next 10 or 15 or 20 years to fill in the gaps.

Obama: Figure out what those linkages will be.

Barry: Right. Make sure there is accountability up and down, and that's probably the toughest job . . . .

Joravsky: What Heather Booth has to work out — you know, she is emulating the moral majority in terms of building up these mailing lists, phone banks, and what have you. Every year she sponsors a retreat here in Chicago, and they bring in a parade of leading Democratic figures to come in and give speeches. It's a networking session. You get to meet people to work on your campaign and that kind of thing. It's really hard for her to sort of distinguish between an issue like an environmental issue and the reelection of Paul Simon. In effect, her efforts are in both directions. She was very involved in the Harold Washington campaign, too. So she has a problem because a lot of people she wants to organize, a lot of people who are on her side, are not voting for Harold Washington or Paul Simon. That is something she has to wrestle with . . . .

Clark: I was going to say that two of the new leaders I discussed in my story met each other and met with other similar new leaders at the NPA [National Peoples Action] conference in Washington, D.C. And it's sort of, from my way of looking at it, kind of an old, worn-out kind of staging that Gale pulls off every year. Yet, when I heard these people talk about meeting people from Chicago they hadn't been dealing with before and meeting other people from other cities, working on environmental problems, housing problems. It was a very strong, affirming week for them . . . .

Kretzmann: As a form of leadership development in fact.

Clark: An incredibly powerful form of leadership development.

Hallett: Two very quick things, one just to follow up on that. It seems to say that in the days of the Reagan era there weren't a whole lot of places where people could come together, people of like minds. The effect of having a large gathering is important. The other thing that is noticeable — because I went to a Citizen's Action retreat this year — is that it's essentially all white. And that always calls up a whole other set of issues.

Karanja: I have two basic concerns, and Anne [Hallett] hit upon one. Despite what one may think of leadership, one of the most successful and most influential community organizations that has ever been built is TWO [The Woodlawn Organization]. I haven't heard anyone really talk about that. I think that in its initial development TWO was probably the organizing model in terms of utilizing development, utilizing politicians, impacting political activity. TWO was a model, a model nationwide . . . . So what I hear is that we are talking at a level that really does not address many of the issues that communities in deep poverty are facing. The problem of AIDS, the problem of robbery, of how to organize black youth.

The problem of jobs, real jobs. How do we begin to make those things happen?

Clark: I'm glad you raised that. It seems that LeClaire Court's [public housing tenants organization in southwest Chicago] campaign [to get the Chicago Housing Authority and HUD to agree to tenant management] might be an interesting contemporary example of a campaign that was after development, literally and figuratively, and got it. There is obviously a strong leadership development component, and that is something I'm waiting to see get replicated. . . .

Kretzmann: Sokoni [Karanja], can I use your remarks as not only a helpful reminder but a bridge to issues that Bill was dealing with as we get out of Chicago into some very poor areas in the south suburbs?

Kemp: There is no magic line that divides Chicago from the south suburbs. Green lawns and curving streets do not start at Calumet City and Dolton and Blue Island and Harvey. The problems facing those communities are as severe as in some areas of Chicago, and I think people have to come to grips with that. Part of the reason I wrote the article is that the south suburbs are the great untold story. They have 500,000 people there. Demographically, economically, racially and socially, it's probably the most diverse area in the nation, and racial transformation in those areas is unlike anywhere else in the nation. The movement of blacks into those communities is on a scale unlike anywhere right now, bar none. So you can talk about certain areas in Chicago, but the south suburbs are certainly a major model right now.

Unlike Barack and Ben and Thom, I don't come from a community organizing background, so as an outsider I may be able to present a perspective that is different and hopefully a little better perspective, or just hopefully a different perspective, whatever that may mean.

Like I said, some of the south suburban areas, Blue Island, Robbins, Harvey, Phoenix, Chicago Heights, are the poorest suburbs in the nation. And I think community organizing nationally, as well as in Cook County, has to address the question of the underclass, the poorest of the poor, mainly black. It hasn't really done that yet. I went to Ford Heights, the poorest neighborhood in the country allegedly. If you want to go in there to organize, there are no churches, no youth groups, no labor unions, no nuclear and no extended families. There are no jobs. So what do you do there?

I think the underclass is the great issue of the late '80s and '90s that the country has to deal with. And [President] Bush is infuriating by talking about the war on drugs, as Reagan did in '86. It's not a war on drugs, it's another war on poverty that we need, and everybody kind of backs away, referring to Shriver and Johnson and Kennedy, saying, "We have already done that. It doesn't work."

You can't address drugs without addressing the larger problems of housing, unemployment, single-parent families. They're all intertwined.

And I think that's an avenue where community organizing can enter and possibly do something. The federal government sure doesn't seem to be interested right now, neither does the state government.

Obama: It's not just an underclass that seems to cut off at a certain point — I know that's not how you're using the term. There's a slide. There is this big slippery slope of folks and communities that are sinking. The question is: What can organizing do about helping them, first, to stem the tide and then to build back up? . . . How do you link up some of the most important lessons about organizing — accountability, training, leadership and that stuff — with some powerful messages that came out of the civil rights movement or what Jesse Jackson has done or what's been done by other charismatic leaders? A whole sense of hope is generated out of what they do.

Jesse Jackson can go into these communities and get these people excited and inspired. The organizational framework to consolidate that is missing. The best organizers in the black community right now are the crack dealers. They are fantastic. There's tremendous entrepreneurship and skill. So when I talk about vision or culture it has to do with how organizing in those communities can't just be instrumental. It can't just be civic. It can't just be "Let's get power, call in the alderman, etc." It has to be recreating and recasting how these communities think about themselves.

Kemp: The problem is exacerbated in the south suburbs. There is not a sense that we belong to the city of Chicago. The Chicago Area Project is working in Chicago Heights, and they are dealing just in Chicago Heights with different school districts and different municipalities and park districts. Part of the problem I tried to address in the article was the difficulty of organizing the suburbs. But apart from that is what Paul said, that unfortunately the working class always bears the brunt of the forefront of integration. I don't even like the term "integration." I haven't seen it yet. It's not Winnetka. It's not Hinsdale. It's Calumet City and Harvey and Blue Island. The term I've heard is there is a — the whites in the south suburbs, some of the working-class areas, are making a wagon trail to northwest Indiana, Merrillville, which — funny enough — was a community that was created from the white flight from Gary . . . .

Green: He raises a critical question, but part of it is philosophical, and part of it has to do with the purpose of this conference. Most of the people involved in community organizing are from the left to the far left to beyond the left. They have a notion of how society should operate. Those of us who are familiar with the south suburbs, where our university [Governors State] is located, have done extensive research . . . . What you're looking at are problems that are beyond the liberal or radical orientation. These people are not closet socialists; they are raw capitalists. They want jobs. They want to get part of the system. These are the most noun-and-verb people I have ever met in my life. They want to know specific stuff, how it's going to work.

Karanja: I think that we make a mistake when we think that we cannot organize in the very poorest communities. I think that's the kind of propaganda that has been put out there. I mean, when you talk about the term, "underclass," you create a phenomenon that can't really be dealt with. And that's not true. If you look at the farmers in Mississippi who took the lead in the civil rights movement — back in the '20s and '30s, they were dirt-poor people. But, you know, taking the long view of that, at the point when the civil rights organizers came in, the farmers were the ones who could come out because they had control of their land. They were a part of a land-grant system that had been put into place 20 or 30 years before. So when you think about organizing in situations where there are very few resources, you have to look at what you can do immediately and at what you can do in the long term — how you build people. How do you hook it up with what Jesse is talking about, with what the local minister may be talking about? . . .

This is brief. I think we need to disabuse ourselves of this kind of thinking, and that is that race is not an issue. Race is always an issue . . . . It's always operating at some level in the minds of the groups that are interacting. It's always there. What happens when groups are able to move together is that they face that fact and deal with it in some kind of constructive or compromising way. That's the only way it happens. Race is an issue at all times in this country.

Kretzmann: Okay. Thank you. I don't want us to leave without giving Cheryl [Frank] and Christopher [Reed] a moment here. Cheryl is talking about organizing downstate.

Frank: I think the reporting that I did for the downstate article can be viewed a little differently from what the other authors had to do because it was such a diverse thing to look at, so many different inspiring people to get to know, most of whom never ended up in my article. There was just so much you could say.

But I want you to know that Chicago organizers seem to have discovered downstate at some point. Now, I think the reason they did that was because they figured out there was money downstate, and they figured out there were votes downstate. They figured out there were people downstate, white people and minorities, to deal with and form alliances with and go to the legislature and get some things they wanted and play off other groups that were against them. Some of the people who discovered downstate include Shel Trapp and NTIC [National Training and Information Center].

There is also Dewayne Readus [leader of the Hay Homes Tenants Rights Association in Springfield]. He may not be the coolest guy to a lot of middle-class people or lawmakers who aren't used to dealing with him or to many of us who aren't used to dealing with certain rhetoric, certain issues, but I think he is pretty cool. He set up a little radio station in the projects there, and he didn't get the proper license, but he is beaming his message around to everybody within a several-block area. Talk about the media, there is an embyronic media going on there. Whether he will be able to continue doing that or not, I don't know.

He also helped to lead the [voting rights] demonstrations in Springfield, as I tried to bring out in my article . . . . He did this in conjunction with someone whom he knew as an enemy, who I think is also pretty neat, Alderman Frank McNeil, one of the first black aldermen elected in Springfield. In combination with other forces, McNeil and Readus, and many other hard-working, thoughtful people, and James Craven and Don Craven, who headed up the law firm that brought up the voting rights lawsuit in Springfield, transformed the city government there.

So that's an example of how people with different philosophies, from different walks of life — they don't have the dogmas about what's right and wrong — they just know they have some people they are trying to deal with. They want to see more equality, and they want to see changes in the way the police relate to the black community, for example. They want to see changes in the education given to black people so that black people can advance.

Another person who discovered downstate a long time ago is Bob Creamer of IPAC [Illinois Public Action Council]. He often consults with the various community organizing people affiliated with IPAC. As you know, it's gotten to be quite a network downstate. They do hope to become the Democratic party or at least the balancing portion of the Democratic party. I think they want to control state government at some time in the future. I don't know whether that will ever happen . . . . I think one reason that Bob Creamer discovered downstate was because, first of all, it can be a testing ground. He could find out what does work. I think there has been a testing ground going on for quite a few years before they settled into their current pattern, which I won't attempt to describe completely, but I think you all are familiar with.

I think another reason that Bob Creamer discovered downstate was because of Heather Booth [director of Midwest Academy in Chicago]. She influenced Mike Doyle, who set up the Champaign County Health Care Consumers there, and they [Health Care Consumers] are getting into reforming the dental system so that poor people can get dental care. They are into saying, "Hey, Carle Clinic, you are supposed to have HMO coverage, yet you charge people $50 every time they go to the doctor, and you are charging us co-payments. That's completely away from the HMO concept you sold us on." They are looking for issues that cut across race and cut across class and education. I think they have been pretty successful.

And Jim Duffett is another one who organizes well. And so is John Lee Johnson, who has been a community leader in Champaign-Urbana all his life practically. He is a black man there who is very influential in his community. They have all formed alliances. They are all working together. Jim Duffett worked in Danville for a couple of years on utility issues, and he worked with labor groups. As you know, Danville is a strong labor community . . . .

Let me touch on a couple of other things. A community to watch in the media and get to know about is Cairo. You probably remember there were very polarized racial relationships down there . . . . And it really came to a head in the '60s and '70s. There was a boycott of white businesses because the blacks could not make any inroads. Well, there is a man there [community developer and retired Southern Illinois University professor Richard Poston] who is trying to change things.

Either through force of personality — some people would say because he is charismatic, but also because the leaders there are charismatic, like Angela Greenwell from the community, and many other people — they are trying to transform Cairo and to make it a tourist attraction by building up the riverfront. They want to bring in jobs and economic development, and they are running into a stumbling block because the mayor and others in the city council and the power structure feel threatened by this.

Something to watch for is a book that Ron Powers is writing. He is a national journalist and media critic . . . . He's writing a book about Cairo. What happened, why it happened, what succeeded and what didn't. He is comparing Cairo, which has been on a downward slide, with another city that has blossomed overnight. He is trying to figure out why one community took off and the other didn't.

The last thing I want to leave you with is this: There is a lot of cross-pollination going on downstate. They aren't arguing about — "Well, I like Gale Cincotta." "No, I like Heather Booth." "I'm a socialist." "No, I'm not. I just want jobs or whatever." And so they are able to take from these various traditions and use them in their community to do what needs to get done. I think that's a good idea. I think there are a multitude of models. There are a multitude of approaches to a problem. There are traditional approaches which should not be overlooked.

Eventually the people in all these community groups end up at the State Capitol looking for legislation. The black farmers of Pembroke did that. They are trying to get legislation passed to help them document where these high-capacity wells are. They say the irrigators are taking the water from their lands so they can't use their wells or grow their crops. So far they haven't gotten the legislation they want passed, but they are going back for the veto session.

There are a lot of activities. It's very diverse. There is a lot of cross-pollination and mentoring going on. I think that there might be some lessons to learn from downstate . . . .

Delgado: As far as the interest downstate, I would say that, in fact, [without downstate] you are not going to get anything passed in the state legislature . . . .

Frank: That's right. They know they need political power . . . .

Delgado: I would like to see more of the downstate-Chicago connection and more federal legislation that puts decisionmaking capability at the local and state level.

Frank: I think it's going to be something to watch . . . .

Kretzmann: . . . . Christopher, your piece ended the series and reminded us of how different this city has been since the Washington years and how the relationships between community organizations, particularly in the black community, growing out of the rich civic life of the black community on the south side and west side, got changed by the shift in City Hall.

Reed: . . . . There is a civic tradition that goes back into the 19th century, and there were politicians coming from the heart of black Chicago politics from the south side who linked up not only to the political activities that were going on, but also to the civic tradition. I think that explains Harold Washington.

So what I wanted to do was to look at what Harold Washington said, and I assumed he meant what he said. Upon examination, I found out what he said was in fact what he wanted to do. What did Harold Washington say, and what did Harold Washington do? What he did was something quite unusual. Of course, not so unusual for a true reformer, which is what he was, out of the old Hyde Park tradition . . . . I am talking about the Charles Merriam tradition. The senior. Going back to the turn of the century. Then his son [Robert] later, who ran against [Richard J.] Daley in 1955.

There were several traditions that Harold Washington could have tapped into — and he did. The odd thing is he did not have to become a believer in bedrock democracy. He came from a petty bourgeoisie background. He attended private school in Milwaukee. After service [in World War II] he went to Roosevelt University, and then he went to Northwestern. At his death he was not in a black community, but in Hyde Park.

And for whatever reasons — and it has to be explored later; I won't even bring the question up because this is something that needs to be explored in the character of the man — he chose to align himself with ordinary folk and their aspirations. Obviously, he got votes from them, but it was much more than that. He did attempt to do that which they needed most: empower them.

Politics does play a part; race plays a part. Politics plays a part because we are talking about power. And here, all of a sudden, someone says, "I am going to extend my hand to you, and you can energize from me, and you can do things on your own." From what he said it appears it worked. From what I saw it appeared it worked. So I wrote it up that way.

I looked at four organizations [The Woodlawn Organization (TWO),

Kenwood Oakland Community Organization (KOCO), Midwest Community Council and Bethel New Life], and all of the leaders of those organizations talked about how after Washington came into power there was, in fact, greater energy to do what needed to be done. That was very important.

The organizations that were empowered are organizations that are all led by people who have a grass-roots connection. There are block club meetings, conventions from all the organizations. They do have a grass-roots following. There is power out there, and they have built upon the key resource that you need in any area. And that key resource is what? Hope. Raised expectations translate into hope, and then you can move on. That's what you need. The first thing is hope.

TWO is a great example of how an organization can work black on black, but so is Bethel New Life under Mary Nelson, so is Midwest Community Council under Nancy Jefferson. KOCO attempts the same thing . . . . I think what I have written speaks for what can be done in areas that are either filled with people who are very poor or that are mixed areas. The Bethel attempt to upgrade West Garfield Park and part of Austin involves Bethel not only with people who are in the underclass, but also people who are working class, working poor, and people who are part of the petty bourgeoisie, because Bethel has in fact provided housing for all of those classes of people.

All of the organizations, by the way, address the concerns that you talked about. TWO is concerned with crime prevention; it is concerned with addiction to alcohol and drugs, and so is Midwest Community Council. They are all involved in school reform, and they are all involved in housing. Those are comprehensive programs that these groups are building.

Obama: Chris raised an interesting issue: the relationship between what was an essentially charismatic leader, Harold Washington, and the process of organizing. It strikes me that Harold Washington did benefit from that plowing of the soil that took place in the black community, that his election was an expression of a lot of organizing that had been taking place over a long time. I would also agree that to a large extent he wanted to give back to that process. He wanted to give those groups recognition and empower them in some sense.

What is interesting, and I don't know whether this came out — but my experience working here possibly shows itself — is that I am not sure how well those links were maintained over the course of the administration, what kinds of pressures were brought to bear in terms of maintaining those links between organizing and the administration.

What I mean by that is this: Harold Washington did open up the door to a lot of the organizations and minorities. What would have been real empowerment was not done. And I think what was unfortunate, was that Harold Washington instead of actually just getting contacts back or instead of just bringing them into the board room, [should have been] helping to foster in the black community the sense that they need to organize even more and build even more and broaden their base.

Reed: He did that.

Obama: I'm not sure . . . . I think he made an effort. Any time that you recognize these groups, you are saying that this kind of activity is legitimate, and that I am going to deal with it. I think that is empowerment, but you do get a sense that more of that might have been done.

Reed: I think everything that could have been done was done. And, in fact, had he attempted to personally inject himself in, say, West Garfield or East Garfield or wherever, this would have been found to be objectionable. What he did was all that he should have done, and those groups were quite capable of doing what they had to do on their own.

Remember now, after Washington died, Sawyer was pressured by the constituents of these groups to continue the Washington legacy, which is what Sawyer did.

Barry: I thoroughly agree with you that Harold Washington changed the system, and I think a lot of it is change that you can't go back on. One of the things he brought, not to the black community so much as to the industrial community, he started funding the industrial development groups around the city. He gave them funding to work locally to develop industry. There have been rumblings that [Mayor Richard M.] Daley will pull that money back, but I don't think so because this method works. Washington knew that if he put the power out there, it would work.

Reed: That's it. The Squires book [*Race, Class and the Response to Urban Decline*], the book on Chicago. Washington's presence by 1983 answers the question: Can you expect a future for the ordinary people? The answer became yes . . . .

Karanja: You also have to look at where Washington got his mandate. I mean, it was not politicians that got him into this. It was community groups that said, first of all, we want you. And then, secondly, we are going to deliver the funds to make it happen.

Reed: That's right. He owed the community groups . . . . I will say beyond that, that Harold Washington was more than just a politician. The First Congressional District was probably the best cradle for learning politics or one of the best in the nation . . . . But I think the point is there is more to Washington than just the politician. I am saying there was a true reformer, a man who turned his back on community groups who made inordinate demands that he didn't think were morally right, intellectually sound or whatever. I know people who said, "Boy, you're a hard person to deal with. Doesn't he understand what we want?"

Yes, he understood. He said that wouldn't be fair for the city so he turned them down. He was an extraordinary man . . . .

Hallett: I guess I agree that he was a real reformer, and I think as far as organizing goes, it's as though we were just getting beyond the honeymoon when he died . . . . Again, around the education stuff, I did not like how he handled the teachers' strike. I think it was just about to get interesting. And groups that were being asked to stop beating up on City Hall and take a place at the table were about to really get comfortable at the table and enter into a rich and developmental stage for community organizing in Chicago. Then all of a sudden everything got swept away again. So it felt like we were going to move into a very rich and new time that would have had all sorts of possibilities.

Obama: . . . . The concern that I have is that Harold Washington did empower a lot of groups, but the problem is that there were huge bald spots in terms of where that power was. I think KOCO and Nancy Jefferson's group, and a whole range of groups — TWO — do have some very solid organizations. Where I was working on the far south side or in some of the housing projects, you have communities that had not experienced that building up process in terms of the organizing, that didn't have the sort of ligaments and structure that allowed them to deal with the city. So you had a range of these constituents that he was looking after from a politician's perspective. But they didn't necessarily have the capacity to articulate their needs. If they were brought to the table, a lot of times their agendas would be lost or manipulated, or what have you, not necessarily by him, but by the various forces because it was a big table and there were a lot of folks around it.

I am not saying that was Harold Washington's responsibility. I think what I was trying to lift up was the fact that when you have a charismatic leader, whether it's Jesse Jackson or Harold Washington or what have you, there has to be some sort of interaction that helps to feed back and move back all that energy into the community to build up more organizing. He tried to do that. All I am saying is that more of that needs to be done.

Reed: Let me just respond to that. Bedrock democracy rested upon the people themselves, pulling themselves up. All Washington had to do was what he did . . . . What he did was substantial in that people in the communities felt, "Well, now, we can do more for ourselves and face fewer obstacles down at City Hall." . . . That's what he was supposed to do as a governmental leader. The people themselves, however, white, brown, black, whatever, have to do something on their own. That's bedrock democracy . . . .

Joravsky: I want to clarify something I said earlier in terms of organizing poor people. I think you can organize poor people, but you can't rebuild poor communities either in Chicago or downstate unless you get some kind of assistance from the outside, be it federal assistance, be it private enterprise — anybody. You have to have some money.

Frank: That's true . . . .

Obama: Along that same note, coming out of this discussion and certainly what I have been thinking about since I left Developing Communities Project is that organizing should be a bridge in a whole range of ways. Organizing offers the possibility of being a bridge between ideologies that I mentioned earlier. It isn't a matter of self-help versus handouts. It's a matter of creating a dynamic where people help themselves and are also helped and may help others. It's that organizing can expand that community and foster communication between various groups.

Organizing can also be a bridge between the private and the public, between politics and people's everyday lives. If organizing is effective, it shows people that what they go through every day — the hard knocks, the frustrations, the difficulties — is in some way linked up with what other people are going through and with what they read in the newspapers. So that what they do in their own lives will have an impact on what happens in newspapers, what happens in elections and what happens in their communities.

Green: I'm a person who has fought for a long time against teaching community organizations to poor people as a college course. I was much more involved in teaching accounting and hard skills so they wouldn't need a community organizer to tell them what to do. They could do it for themselves. That's a personal, philosophical belief that I have, and I still believe that.

You could hear from what I said that I am not necessarily sold on community organizing as a substitute for individual decisionmaking. I still believe individual decisionmaking is far better. I think we have seen a diminution of the internal building blocks of our society: the family, education, the church .... and I think the external group — the politicians, the unions, the media — have basically abdicated their responsibility .... The last point I want to make is that all of this would be irrelevant if there was economic viability, if people could take care of their own lives. I think the problem rests far less in community organizing and far more in individuals getting the kind of education whereby they don't need anyone to tell them how, when or what to do.

Reed: I agree with most of this. I must say that I'm a little more optimistic than Paul.

Green: Almost everybody is.

Reed: Let me say this: I agree with you, except I don't think education is the way out. I think what we need is a redistribution of power. The reality of, say, fighting redlining is that — what was it? — the money was too expensive once it was made available? That doesn't surprise me. The word dialectic was used. Well, there is an antithesis between what community organizers want to do and what the people in power don't want to happen. I mean, there is a normal clash. Despite all that, I am optimistic that the average person, wherever he or she is found, can make some change at some level.

I do agree with Green. There are tremendous obstacles, but I am still optimistic. I think what we have seen at the national level since Roosevelt's New Deal, has helped people arrive at a point where they think they can do more for themselves and can as individuals, as members of groups tap into whatever opportunities there are.

Karanja: . . . . The other piece of it is, I think, in poor communities — I am talking particularly about black communities — we approach it from trying to organize block clubs, that kind of thing, and creating leaders and that kind of thing. I think all of that is necessary, but ultimately what we really need to address in a community like Robbins, in the south suburbs and Grand Boulevard and some parts of the west side, is that we need to build. We need to build infrastructure that does not exist, has not existed. There has to be created a model not unlike the models that exist in developing countries. That means that we can't look at this as something we can do in two years, three years. We have to look at 10 or 20 years out.

The other piece that is critical is that there has to be a value base in this kind of organizing and community building that is very different from what is currently going on. It can't just be getting a piece of the pie. There has to be more concern for one's fellow man and fellow woman. That is what is missing in our organizing effort. You know, we fight them and we win. It's not just winning for me. It's that we all come along, that we all grow and we all move, that we build something that is going to last. . . .

Barry: I think we have all been saying pretty much the same thing. Organizing is a developing science of enormous importance. The way I think of it, the most important thing is we have got a world that will have 10 billion people on it, and if we don't organize that world, it's going to blow up in our faces. I think organizing is like politics, like business. It's part of the way this world is going to be managed over the long haul.

Kemp: In my closing comment in the context of the underclass — and if you don't like the term "underclass," use another term — but it's out there and growing, and if it's not the most important issue right now, it will be in the '90s.

If you are going to organize in the community, you need some type of structure there, whether in the community, the family or the individual. For the first time in large-sized communities, you don't have that anymore. Families are collapsing, and partially it's due to race and other things — we don't need to get into that — but the black youths in Harvey, Blue Island, Altgeld Gardens, Robbins, the Hay Homes in Springfield deserve a lot better, and they are not getting it. I don't think community organizing right now has the tools to address their problems.

[Sokoni Karanja] mentioned that you need to build an infrastructure. I think that's right. Addressing PCBs in the neighborhoods, fine. Environmental problems. Housing. But it always comes down to whether that individual has family support and a job. If community organizing can succeed in presenting those two things, it will do a lot more than it has done in the last two decades or so.

For Further Reading

T his reading list includes books and articles on a host of topics: Saul Alinsky, Richard Poston, ethnic and minority groups in the U.S. and Illinois, civil rights organizing, church-based organizing, the role of ideology, art as a form of organizing, farm and environmental organizing, Chicago school reform, neighborhood economic development, industrial retention, and neighborhood organizations and political movements. When possible, the specific Illinois subject is noted. From this list it is evident that downstate Illinois and rural areas in general are not as well-represented in organizing literature as they should be. The suburbs get equally short shrift, an indication — since there's plenty to write about — that the activity there is not getting beyond the daily newspapers. But Chicago is cited again and again. In 1990 as in 1939, it is a still a laboratory of civic action for the nation, a place where the big stories begin.

Abbott, Philip. 1986. *Seeking Many Inventions: The Idea of Community in America.* Knoxville: University of Tennessee.

Anderson, Alan B., George W. Pickering. 1986. *Confronting the Color Line: The Broken Promise of the Civil Rights Movement in Chicago.* Athens: The University of Georgia Press.

Alinsky, Saul, D. 1945. *Reveille for Radicals.* Chicago: University of Chicago Press.

_____. *Rules for Radicals.* 1972. New York: Vintage.

Association of Chinese from Indo China (now the Southeast Asia Center). 1985. "Why Americans act and think strangely, or why Indo-Chinese act and think strangely," New Life News, 2:1, 1-7. Southeast Asia Center, Chicago.

Bachelor, Lynn Wheeler. 1976. *The Community Organization as a Political Representative* (NCO). Ph.D. dissertation, University of Chicago.

Bailey, Robert Jr. 1981. *Radicals in Urban Politics: The Alinsky Approach* (Organization for a Better Austin, 1968-1971). Chicago: University of Chicago Press.

Bean, Frank and Marta Tienda. 1987. *Hispanic Population of the United States.* New York: Russell Sage Foundation.

Bennett, Michael. 1990, March. "A prediction: Chicago won't go the way of New York," *Catalyst: Voices of Chicago's School Reform,* 1:2, 12-13.

_____. *Devolving Roles and Structures of Community Organizations: Social Action, Social Service, and Economic Development.* Unpublished Ph.D. dissertation, University of Chicago.

Berger, Peter L. and Richard J. Neuhaus. 1977. *To Empower People: The Role of Mediating Structures in Public Policy.* Washington, D.C.: American Enterprise Institute.

Betten, Neil and Michael J. Austin, contributions by Robert Fisher. 1990. *The Roots of Community Organizing: 1917-1939.* Philadelphia: Temple University Press.

Boyte, Harry C. 1980. *The Backyard Revolution: Understanding the New Citizens Movement.* Philadelphia: Temple University Press.

_____. 1984. *Community is Possible.* New York: Harper and Row.

_____. 1989. *Commonwealth.* New York: Free Press.

_____. 1989. "Moving into Power: Reinvigorating Public Life in the 1990s," *Occasional Papers,* Chicago: Community Renewal Society.

_____ and Sara Evans. 1986. *Free Spaces: The Sources of Democratic Change in America.* New York: Harper & Row.

_____ and Frank Reissman, eds. 1986. *The New Populism: The Politics of Empowerment.* Philadelphia: Temple University Press.

_____, Heather Booth and Steve Max. 1986. *Citizen Action and the New American Populism.* Philadelphia: Temple University Press.

Branch, Taylor. 1989, May. "Blacks and Jews: The Uncivil War (Chicago)," *Esquire,* 89-90, 92, 94, 96, 105-106, 108, 110, 114, 116.

Braser, George. 1987. *Community Organizing.* New York: Columbia University Press.
Brazier, Arthur M. 1969. *Black Self-Determination: The Story of the Woodlawn Organization.* Grand Rapids: Eerdmans.
Bruyn, Severyn T. and James Meehan, eds. 1987. *Beyond the Market and the State: New Directions in Community Development.* Philadelphia: Temple University Press.
Burghardt, Stephen. 1982. *The Other Side of Organizing.* Cambridge, Mass.: Schenkman Publishing Company; Beverly Hills, Cal.: Sage Publishing Company, Human Services Guide, #27.
Calumet Project for Industrial Jobs (community organizations, churches, unions, economists in Indiana and Illinois). 1989. *Preventing Plant Closings in Northwest Indiana.* East Chicago: Calumet Project.
Camacho, Eduardo and Ben Joravsky. 1989. *Against the Tide: The Middle Class in Chicago.* Chicago: Community Renewal Society.
Casuso, Jorge and Eduardo Camacho. 1985. *Hispanics in Chicago.* The Chicago Reporter and the Community Renewal Society.
Castenada, Ruben. 1988, January. "Community organizers bring new clout to urban poor (IAF organizing in Los Angeles)," *California Journal,* 21-25.
Chavez, Cesar E. 1974. "The Mexican American and the Church" in F. Chris Garcia, ed. *La Causa Politica: A Chicano Politics Reader.* Notre Dame, Ind.: University of Notre Dame.
Chicago. 1989, July. Special Issue: "The Real Chicago Southside Story" (includes Southwest Community Congress, integration, ethnic and African American neighborhoods).
Chicago. Kim, Bok-Lim. 1975. *A Study of Asian-Americans in Chicago.* Wash., D.C.: National Institutes of Mental Health.
Chicago Community Organization Directory (boundaries, services and publications). 1987. Community Renewal Society: Chicago.
Chicago Reporter. 1989, April. "Minorities Surge in Chicago's Suburban Ring," 1-6, 11.
Cockcroft, Eva, John Weber, James Cockcroft. 1977. *Toward a Peoples Art: The Contemporary Mural Movement* (includes Chicago). New York: E.E. Dutton.
Comstock, Gary. ed. 1988. *Is There a Moral Obligation to Save the Family Farm?* Ames: Iowa State University Press.
Copp, Jay. 1990, March 9, 16, 23. "Cluster Project Promotes Neighborhood Growth, (Southwest Catholic Cluster Project, integration)." *The New World,* 98:10, 1.
Cortes, Ernesto Jr. 1986, July 11. "Organizing the Community (Industrial Areas Foundation)," *The Texas Observer,* 10-16.
_____, Mike Miller, Jim Gittings, Leon Howell, Paul Burks, Pat Speer. 1987, February 2. "The Gospel in the World: Community Organizing (good overview of the different kinds of organizing)," *Christianity and Crisis.* 47:1.
Creamer, Bob. 1983, Spring. "Illinois Public Action Council," *Social Policy,* 23-28.
Cruz, Wilfredo. 1987. *The Nature of Alinsky-Style Community Organizing in the Mexican American Community of Chicago.* Unpublished Ph.D. dissertation, University of Chicago.
Delgado, Gary. 1986. *Organizing the Movement: The Roots and Growth of ACORN.* Philadelphia: Temple University Press.
Denise, Paul S. and Ian M. Harris. 1990. *Experiential Education for Community Development* (international case studies; SIU community development tradition). Westport Conn.: Greenwood Press.
1990 Directory of Community Organizations in Chicago. Institute of Urban Life: Chicago.
DeZutter, Hank. 1989, June. "One Chicago, one neighborhood, one woman's hope (Mary Volpe, Northeast Austin Organization)," *Chicago Reporter,* 8-9, 11.
Durning, Alan B. 1989. *Action at the Grass Roots: Fighting Poverty and Environmental Decline* (a global look at organizing). No. 88, The Worldwatch Paper Series. Washington, D.C.: Worldwatch Institute.
Ecklein, Joan Levin. 1984. *Community Organizers* (includes Alinsky/FIGHT; multi-racial parents councils). New York: Wiley.
Evans, Sara. 1979. *Personal Politics: The Roots of Women's Liberation in the Civil Rights Movement and the New Left.* New York: Random House.
Finks, P. David. 1984. *The Radical Vision of Saul Alinsky.* New York: Paulist Press.
Fish, John. 1973. *Black Power/White Control: The Struggle of the Woodlawn Organization of*

Chicago. Princeton, N.J.: Princeton University Press.
Fisher, Robert. 1984. *Let the People Decide* (critique of Alinsky). Boston: Twayne Publishers.
_____ and Peter Romanofsky, eds. 1981. *Community Organizing for Urban Social Change: A Historical Perspective.* Greenwood, Conn.: Greenwood Press.
_____ and Joseph M. Kling. 1987, January-February. "Leading the People: Two Approaches to the Role of Community Organizing (ideology)." *Radical America,* 21:1, 31-45.
_____. 1989, December. "Community Mobilization: Prospects for the Future," *Urban Affairs Quarterly,* 25:2, 200-211.
Fleming, Thomas J. 1987, April. "The merits of political patronage (voting rights act)," *Illinois Issues,* 8-9.
Flood, Bill. 1984, September/October. "Bringing Life to Communities: Cultural Animation (Bushnell, Illinois)," *Rain,* 14-18.
Frank, Cheryl. 1988, October. "Richard Poston's great plans for Cairo," *Illinois Issues,* 19.
_____. 1989, December. "Jim Craven of voting rights fame," *Illinoi Issuess,* 13-15.
Fremon, David K., 1988. *Chicago Politics Ward by Ward.* Bloomington and Indianapolis: University of Indiana Press.
_____. 1990, January. "Chicago's Spanish-American politics in the '80s." *Illinois Issues,* 16-18.
Garcia, F. Chris, ed. 1988. *Latinos and the Political System* (includes Illinois and the Midwest). Notre Dame, Ind.: University of Notre Dame Press.
Garland, Anne Witte. 1986. *Women Activists: Challenging the Abuse of Power* (Gale Cincotta). New York: Feminist Press, City University of New York.
Getting Connected: How to Find Out About Groups and Organizations in Your Neighborhood (manual based on Logan Square, Chicago). 1989. Evanston: Center for Urban Affairs and Policy Research, Northwestern University.
Giloth, Robert. 1985, Winter. "Organizing for Neighborhood Development (critique of McKnight and Kretzmann)," *Social Policy.* 15:3, 37-42.
_____ and Betancur, J. 1988, Summer. "Where downtown meets neighborhood: industrial displacement in Chicago, 1978-87," *Journal of American Planning Association,* 54:3, 279-290.
Gorov, Lynda. 1989. "Come See What I'm Saying (Bertha Gilke and Chicago tenants' organizations)," *Occasional Papers,* Chicago: Community Renewal Society.
Green, Paul M. and Melvin G. Holli. 1989. *Bashing Chicago Traditions: Harold Washington's Last Campaign.* Grand Rapids, Mich.: Eerdmans.
Haider, Donald. 1986. "Partnerships redefined: Chicago's New Opportunities," *Academy of Political Science Proceedings,* 36: 137-149.
Hallman, Howard W. 1984. *Neighborhoods: Their Place in Urban Life* (activism, preservation, self-determination). Beverly Hills: Sage Publications.
Hampton, Henry and Steve Fayer. 1990. *Voices of Freedom: An Oral History of the Civil Rights Movement from the 1950s through the 1980s.* (the book that the PBS television series *Eyes on the Prize* is based on, includes Chicago events and leaders.) 1990: New York, Bantam.
Henig, Jeffrey R. 1982. *Neighborhood Mobilization: Redevelopment and Response* (Chicago's West Side, Uptown, Belmont-Cragin). New Brunswick, N.J.: Rutgers University Press.
Hess, G. Alfred, Jr. 1979. "Community Organization in Chicago," Chicago: The Wieboldt Foundation.
Holli, Melvin G. and Peter D'A. Jones, eds. 1984. *Ethnic Chicago* (Revised and expanded). Grand Rapids, Mich.: Eerdmans.
Horwitt, Sanford D. 1989. *Let Them Call Me Rebel: Saul Alinsky, His Life and Legacy.* New York: Alfred A. Knopf.
Johnson, Robert M. 1984, January/February. "What's Happening to the Neighborhood Movement?" *Foundation News.*
_____. "How to Evaluate a Neighborhood Organization," 1984, May/June. *Foundation News.*
Joravsky, Ben and Eduardo Camacho. 1986. *Race and Politics in Chicago.* Chicago: Community Renewal Society.
Juarez Robles, Jennifer. 1988, April. "Latinos Face Mayor Race and 1990s with Uncertainty," *Chicago Reporter,* 1, 6-7.
_____. 1988, June, July, August. "Hispanic Poverty," *Chicago Reporter.*
Kahn, Si. 1982. *Organizing: A Guide for Grassroots Leaders* (Appalachian organizer and folk

singer). New York: McGraw-Hill.

Keating, Ann Burkin. 1988. *Building Chicago: Suburban Developers and the Creation of a Divided Metropolis.* New Brunswick, N.J.: Rutgers University Press.

Kelly, Christine Kuehn, Donald C. Kelly, Ed Marciniak. 1988. *Non-Profits with Hard Hats: Building Affordable Housing.* Washington, D.C.: National Center for Urban Ethnic Affairs.

Kopecky, Frank and Crystal Schrof. 1987, August/September. "Voting rights in Lincoln's hometown," *Illinois Issues,* 25-28.

Lancourt, Joan E. 1979. *Confront or Concede: The Alinsky Citizen-Action Organizations* (includes NCO, TWO and CAP). Lexington, Mass.: Lexington Books.

Lee, Charles. 1990, February/March. "Evidence of Environmental Racism (includes Chicago)," *Sojourners,* 23-25.

Lewis, Dan A., Jane A. Grant and Dennis P. Rosenbaum. 1988. *The Social Construction of Reform: Crime Prevention and Community Organizations* (Edgewater, Back of the Yards, Gresham-Chatham, Northwest Neighborhood Federation, Northeast Austin). New Brunswick, N.J.: Transaction Books.

Lucas, Isidro and Luis M. Salces. 1981, February. "Hispanics in Illinois: An unfinished political agenda." *Illinois Issues,* 35, 31.

Matthews, Robert. 1988. *The First Charity: How Philanthropy Can Contribute to Democracy in America.* Cabin John, Maryland: Seven Locks Press.

McClory, Robert. 1981, April 3. "Alinsky lives!" (Organization of the NorthEast), Chicago *Reader.*

McKnight, John and John Kretzmann. 1984, Winter. "Community Organizing in the 80s: Toward a Post-Alinsky Agenda (see Giloth)." *Social Policy,* 14:3.

McNeely, Joseph B. 1984, Winter. "The Challenge of Community Development to Neighborhood Leadership," *Urban Resources,* 1:3.

Melvin, Patricia Mooney. 1986. *American Community Organizations: A Historical Dictionary.* New York: Greenwood Press.

Menefee-Libey, David. 1987. *The State of Community Organizing in Chicago.* Chicago: Community Renewal Society.

Metro Ministry News. 1988-89, Winter. Vol. 5, Nos. 1 and 2 (special double issue on church-based organizations, including Chicago's Religious Coalition to End Racial Violence). ICUIS (Institute on the Church in an Urban Industrial Society), Chicago.

Miller, Alton. 1989. *Harold Washington: The Mayor, The Man.* Chicago: Bonus Books.

_____, ed. 1988. *Climbing a Great Mountain: Selected Speeches of Harold Washington.* Chicago: Bonus Books.

Milofsky, Carl, ed. 1988. *Community Organizations: Studies in Resource Mobilization and Exchange.* New York: Oxford University Press.

Montgomery, John and William Ramsden. 1990. *Churches and Community Organizing* (includes Chicago Interfaith Organizing Project; update and directory). Chicago: ICUIS (Institute for the Church in an Urban Industrial Society).

Morris, Aldon D. 1984. *The Origins of the Civil Rights Movement.* New York: Free Press.

Moskowitz, Eric and Dick Simpson. 1984, Winter. "Experiments in Neighborhood Improvement: Chicago as Laboratory." *Urban Resources,* 1:3.

Nandi, Proshanta. 1980. *Quality of Life of Asian Americans* (in a middle-sized Illinois city). Chicago: Asian American Mental Health Research Center. Also, Springfield: Sangamon State University, 1976.

National Civic Review. 1989, May-June. Special issue on Local Organizations and Community Development.

Orfield, Gary and Ricardo M. Tostado, 1983. "Latinos in Metropolitan Chicago: A Study of Housing and Employment." Chicago: Latino Institute, Monograph Series.

Padilla, Felix M. 1985. *Latino Ethnic Consciousness: The Case of Mexican Americans and Puerto Ricans in Chicago.* Notre Dame, Ind.: University of Notre Dame Press.

_____. 1987. *Puerto Rican Chicago.* Notre Dame, Ind.: Notre Dame Press.

Palmer, Parker. 1989. "Scarcity, Abundance and the Gift of Community," *Occasional Papers.* Chicago: Community Renewal Society.

Persons, Stow. 1987. *Ethnic Studies at Chicago, 1905-1945* (Chicago-style sociology that influenced Clifford Shaw and Saul Alinsky). Urbana and Chicago: University of Illinois Press.

Peterman, William and Sherrie Hannon. 1986, Spring. "Influencing change in gentrifying neighborhoods (Lincoln Park)," *Urban Resources,* 3: 33-36.

Pierce, Gregory F. 1984. *Activism that Makes Sense: Congregations and Community Organizing.* Ramsey, N.J.: Paulist Press; Chicago: Acta Publications.

Pierce, Neal R. and Carol F. Steinbach. *Corrective Capitalism: The Rise of America's Community Development Corporations.* New York: Ford Foundation.

Pinderhughes, Diana. 1987. *Race and Ethnicity in Chicago Politics.* Urbana: University of Illinois Press.

Poston, Richard Waverly. 1950. *Small Town Rennaisance: The Story of the Montana Study.* New York: Harpers.

———. 1962. *Democracy Speaks Many Tongues.* New York: Harper and Row.

———. 1971. *The Gang and the Establishment.* New York: Harper and Row.

———. 1976. *Action Now: A Citizens Guide to Better Communities.* Carbondale: Southern Illinois University Press.

Reed, Christopher Robert. 1987, July. "A century of civics and politics: the Afro-Americans of Chicago." *Illinois Issues,* 32-36.

———. July, 1988. "From cultural hegemony to plurality (book review of Persons)," *Illinois Issues,* 30.

Reissman, Frank. 1967, July-August. "The Myth of Saul Alinsky,"*Dissent.* 14:4, 469-478.

Reitzes, Donald C. and Dietrich C. Reitzes. 1983, February. "Saul Alinsky: A Neglected Source But Promising Resource." *The American Sociologist,* No. 17, 45-56.

———. 1987. "Alinsky in the 1980s: Two Contemporary Chicago Community Organizations (United Neighborhood Organization and Organization of the NorthEast)."*Sociological Quarterly.* 28:2, 281-283.

Rose, Don and Richard Rothstein. April 2, 1974. "The CAP Story: Working Class Reformers" (Citizens Against Pollution, later Citizens Action Program). Chicago *Reader.*

Ross, Fred Sr. 1989. *Axioms for Organizers* (pocketsize). San Francisco: Neighbor to Neighbor Education Fund.

———. 1990. *Conquering Goliath* (Cesar Chavez in the 1950s). Keen, Cal.: United Farm-workers.

Rowe, Jonathon. 1990, January. "Commons Sense (review of Boyte's *Commonwealth), Washington Monthly,* 51-54.

Rubin, Herbert J. and Irene Rubin. 1986. *Community Organizing and Development.* Columbus, Ohio: Merrill Publishers.

Russell, Dick. 1990, Winter. "The Rise of the Grass-Roots Toxics Movement." *The Amicus Journal,* 18-21.

Sakolsky, Ron. 1989, Spring/Summer. "Toward a Participatory Culture: Creating Democracy by Democratizing Creativity," *Our Generation,* 33-50.

Salces, Luis M. and Peter W. Colby. 1980, February. "Manana will be better: Spanish-American Politics in Chicago." *Illinois Issues,* 19-21.

Sanders, Marion K. 1965 (reprinted 1970). *The Professional Radical: Conversations with Saul Alinsky.* New York: Harper and Row.

Schwab, Jim. 1988. *Raising Less Corn and More Hell: Midwestern Farmers Speak Out.* Urbana: University of Illinois Press.

Shereikis, Rich. 1990, January 11-17. "United States vs. WTRA" (Dewayne Readus), *Illinois Times* (Springfield), 15:20, 10-14.

———. 1990, January 25-31. "Readus joins other radio radicals," *Illinois Times,* 15:22, 5.

Simpson, Dick W., ed. 1988. *Chicago's Future in a Time of Change.* Champaign: Stripes Publishing Co.

Slayton, Robert A. 1986. *Back of The Yards: The Making of a Local Democracy.* Chicago: University of Chicago Press.

Sorrentino, Anthony. 1977. *Organizing Against Crime: Redeveloping the Neighborhood* (Chicago Area Project). New York. Human Services Press.

Squires, Gregory D. 1987. *Chicago: Race, Class and the Response to Urban Decline.* Philadelphia: Temple University Press.

Starks, Robert T., 1989, July "Analysis of Jackson and PUSH-Excel fall short (book review)," *Illinois Issues,* 27-28.

_____ and Michael B. Preston. 1990. "Harold Washington and the Politics of Reform in Chicago, 1983-1987," in *Racial Politics: American Cities*. Rufus P. Browning, Dale Rogers Marshall, David H. Tabb, eds. New York: Longman.

Staples, Lee. 1984. *Roots to Power: A Manual for Grassroots Organizing* (ACORN-style). New York: Praeger.

Tienda, Marta and Gary Sandefur. 1988. *Divided Opportunity: Minorities, Poverty and Social Policy*. U. of Wisconsin at Madison Institute for Research on Poverty. New York: Plenum Press.

Trapp, Shel. *The Dynamics of Organizing*. Chicago: National Training and Information Center.

Travis, Dempsey T. 1981. *An Autobiography of Black Chicago* (includes Robert Lucas). Chicago: Urban Research Institute.

Waggoner, Dianna. 1988, April. "Joe Szackos: A Grass Roots Organizer Grows a New Crop of Activists in the Eastern Kentucky Hills,"*Governing*, 34-39.

Walton, John and Luis Salces. 1977. *The Political Organization of Chicago's Latino Communities*. Chicago: Northwestern University.

Warren, Elizabeth. 1979. *Chicago's Uptown: Public Policy, Neighborhood Decay and Citizen Action in an Urban Community*. Chicago: Loyola University Center for Urban Policy.

Wellstone, Paul. 1978. *How the Rural Poor Got Power*. Amherst: University of Massachusetts Press.

Weyr, Thomas. 1988. *Hispanic USA: Assimilation or Separation*. New York: Harper and Row.

Wheeler, Charles N. III. 1986, October. "Racial power struggles in Chicago, Springfield," *Illinois Issues*, 2.

Wilentz, Sean. 1989, December. "Local Hero (review of Horwitt)," *The New Republic*, 30-38.

Williams, Michael R. 1985. *Neighborhood Organizing: Seeds of a New Urban Life*. Westport, Conn.: Greenwood Press.

Up-to-date coverage of community organizing

The best sources of information are local newspapers and the organizations themselves. The latter often have informative newsletters. The following journals and newsletters regularly cover community organizing and nonprofit housing and economic development corporations.

The Alert (national)
Community Information Exchange
1029 Vermont Ave. Suite 710
Washington, D.C. 20005

Campaign for Better Health Care
44 Main Street Suite 208
Champaign IL 61820

CANDO (Chicago Association of
Neighborhood Development Organizations
343 S. Dearborn, Suite 910
Chicago IL 60604

Catalyst: Chicago School Reform
Community Renewal Society
332 South Michigan Avenue
Chicago IL 60604

Chicago Reporter (special focus on
race and poverty)
Community Renewal Society
332 South Michigan Ave.
Chicago IL 60604

Citizen Action News (national)
Citizen Action Fund
P.O. Box 33304
Washington, D.C. 20033-3304

CMW Community Media Workshop:
Newstips (Chicago)
Malcolm X College
1900 W. Van Buren
Chicago IL 60612

Community Matters (neighborhood
development)
Community Workshop on
Economic Development
100 S. Morgan
Chicago IL 60607

The CRA Reporter (low-income
neighborhoods)
Center for Community Change
1000 Wisconsin Avenue, NW
Washington, D.C. 20007

Cultural Democracy
(community-based art)
Alliance for Cultural Democracy
P.O. Box 7591
Minneapolis MN 55407

Disclosure (Chicago and national)
National Training and information Center
810 N. Milwaukee Ave.
Chicago IL 60622

Land Stewardship Letter
(sustainable farming, Midwest)
Land Stewardship Project
14578 Ostlund Trail North
Marine MN 55047

Metro Ministry News (Chicago, national)
ICUIS
4750 N. Sheridan, Suite 327
Chicago IL 60640

The Neighborhood Works
(Chicago and national,
organizing and development)
Center for Neighborhood Technology
2125 West North Avenue
Chicago IL 60647

The Network Builder (housing issues,
Chicago and national)
Chicago Rehab Network
53 West Jackson
Chicago IL 60604

Notes from Illinois South
(farms, mines, environment)
Illinois South Project
116 1/2 West Cherry St.
Herrin IL 62948

The Organizer (west coast, national)
Organize Training Center
1095 Market St. 3419
San Francisco, CA 94103

PICO Update (California, national)
Institute for Community Organizations
171 Santa Rosa Ave.
Oakland CA 94610

Reader (neighborhood news column, articles)
11 East Illinois
Chicago IL 60611

Social Policy (organizing and issues, national)
25 West 43rd Street
New York, NY 10036

Statewide Housing Action Coalition
(low-income housing, tenants rights,
statewide)
220 S. State St., Suite 800
Chicago IL 60604

Index